Open Your Third Eye

Ultimate Guide to Open Your Third Eye and Awaken Your Chakras to Enhance Psychic Abilities and Decalcify Pineal Gland

Lisa Blake

© Copyright 2020 by Lisa Blake. All rights reserved.

The work contained herein has been produced with the intent to provide relevant knowledge and information on the topic described in the title for entertainment purposes only. While the author has gone to every extent to furnish up to date and true information, no claims can be made as to its accuracy or validity as the author has made no claims to be an expert on this topic. Notwithstanding, the reader is asked to do their own research and consult any subject matter experts they deem necessary to ensure the quality and accuracy of the material presented herein.

This statement is legally binding as deemed by the Committee of Publishers Association and the American Bar Association for the territory of the United States. Other jurisdictions may apply their own legal statutes. Any reproduction, transmission or copying of this material contained in this work without the express written consent of the copyright holder shall be deemed as a copyright violation as per the current legislation in force on the date of publishing and subsequent time thereafter. All additional works derived from this material may be claimed by the holder of this copyright.

The data, depictions, events, descriptions and all other information forthwith are considered to be true, fair and accurate unless the work is expressly described as a work of fiction. Regardless of the nature of this work, the Publisher is exempt from any responsibility of actions taken by the reader in conjunction with this work. The Publisher acknowledges that the reader acts of their own accord and releases the author and Publisher of any responsibility for the observance of tips, advice, counsel, strategies and techniques that may be offered in this volume.

TABLE OF CONTENTS

INTRODUCTION 1

Chapter 1 *The Third Eye* 3

    Location and Function of Your Third Eye 3

    Correspondences of the Third Eye 5

    Responsibilities of the Third Eye 6

Chapter 2 *Symptoms Of A Blocked Third Eye* 8

    Key Characteristics of the Third Eye Chakra 8

Chapter 3 *Benefits Of A Healthy Third Eye* 12

Chapter 4 *Methods For Opening Your Third Eye* 14

    Yoga for Opening the Third Eye 17

    Affirmations for Opening the Third Eye 17

    Color for Opening the Third Eye 19

Chapter 5 *The Third Eye Doorway To The Psychic World* 21

    Psychic Readings with Mediums 21

    Relaxation, Emptiness, and Meditation 23

    Psychic Sense with Automatic Writing 26

    Psychic Power with Extrasensory Perception (ESP) 29

    The Eight Limbs of Mind Yoga 30

Chapter 6 *Consciousness Of The Third Eye* 34

    The Third Eye States of Consciousness 34

    Third Eye Etheric Vision 36

    The Third Eye and Temporal Vision 38

    Third Eye Spirituality and Mysticism 38

    Third Eye Psychic Visions 40

    The Tunnel of the Third Eye 42

    Telepathic Awareness 43

Chapter 7 *Astral Beings And The Third Eye* **45**

    Other Worlds 45

    Traveling the Astral Planes 46

    Out of Body Experiences 47

    Dream Control 50

Chapter 8 *Spiritual Beings And The Third Eye* **53**

    Earthbound Spirits 53

    Knowing your Spirit Guide 54

    Earth Angel 57

    Divination 58

    Precognition and Spirituality 60

    Etheric Entities on the Physical Plane 61

Chapter 9 *Life After Life* **63**

    Elevated Souls on Earth 63

    Daydreams for Life 64

    Dreaming and Symbolism 67

    Awareness of the Aura 68

    Seeing into the Afterlife 69

    Reincarnation 70

Chapter 10 *Improved Life With An Open Third Eye* **72**

Conclusion **76**

Description 77

INTRODUCTION

Congratulations on purchasing this book, and thank you for doing so.

The following chapters will discuss your Third Eye and its ability to bring power and enlightenment to your life. The mind's window to the universe and all of its power is located in the Third Eye. With an open Third Eye, you will have access to the knowledge of millions of souls that have gone on before, those who now inhabit the astral planes beyond your current field of vision. When the Third Eye is functioning, your brain will flood with light from the universe, and the details of your life will suddenly become clear to you. Your reality will change in ways you never dreamed were possible.

The power of your Third Eye drives all of your intuition and sixth sense. The people and events in your world will suddenly become clear. When you open your Third Eye to the possibilities around you, your inner vision will clear. You will know a new reality that is elevated far above anything you currently know. Your thoughts will be clear and valid. You will know your true inner feelings, and you will make them work for you.

The human mind and spirit are amazing things, but most people are so far removed from realizing their true potential. The real power lies in the Third Eye, and opening it will bring marvelous enlightenment. This enlightenment gives you the ability to know things you could not know before and see something you previously only dreamed about experiencing. This enlightenment will take you to Nirvana, where you will enjoy total peace and contentment. Until you reach this state, you are limited in what you can do and know, but when your Third Eye is functioning, you will achieve all of these things and more.

The abilities that all humans possess are still not understood by most. Conscious thought is one example of this. When a decision is made, and action follows, that action is tainted by the conscious and subconscious mind's knowledge. Every reaction you have to any life event is driven by all your previous life experiences' cumulative effects. Your subconscious will take over when you do not have the time to rationalize the situation. When you have the time to think logically, you can decide on a course of action based on reason and fact. Too often, the subconscious mind takes over and drives your actions.

When your Third Eye is open, your mind will no longer be at war with itself. It will no longer be forced to choose between the conscious facts and the subconscious reasons that drive its actions. When your mind vibrates with the positive energy that comes with an open Third Eye, you will achieve the best possible decisions based on knowledge without discounting your feelings. Your conscious and subconscious minds will merge into one.

The influx of positive energy from the universe will enlighten your mind and create a spiritual transformation that will enable you to achieve true self-realization. Your Third Eye will awaken your intuition and psychic powers that are now lying unused inside you. You will possess insight that goes far beyond any everyday rational thinking you are currently used to knowing. Once you are willing to accept this transformation, there will no longer be limits on anything you wish to achieve.

There are plenty of books on the market on this subject; thanks again for choosing this one! Every effort was made to ensure it is full of as much useful information as possible; please enjoy!

CHAPTER 1
The Third Eye

One of the seven internal chakras is the Third Eye Chakra. It is the esoteric and mystical concept of the invisible, all-knowing eye, usually depicted as centered in the middle of the human forehead. The Third Eye will enable you to have a level of perception that goes far beyond ordinary sight. Ancient philosophers taught that the Third Eye was the location of the seat of your soul.

Location and Function of Your Third Eye
All people have the Third Eye, and everyone can access the powers of their own Third Eye if they choose to. Some people will use it with more intensity and more regularly than other people will. If you feel a feeling in your gut, that little nagging feeling that something isn't quite right, then you are collecting perceptions of the situation from your Third eye. These feelings are quite valid even if you cannot locate the source of information to justify your opinions with facts. Think of your Third Eye as a sense organ with unique powers that can be sharpened and improved with work. Your Third Eye will also help you read the signals from your environment and access your intuition to know the path you need to follow. It will also allow you to tune into the vibrations that come from other people. Strengthening your Third Eye use will help you connect with those whose energies match yours, and it will enhance your perceptions of life.

The Third Eye is the sixth internal chakra. It is referred to as the inner eye, the brow chakra, or the Third Eye Chakra. In Sanskrit, the word for the Third Eye is Ajna. This chakra determines how you evaluate your attitudes and beliefs as it correlates to your psychological skills and mental abilities. Located midway between your eyes, this gland is connected physically to your pineal gland, pituitary gland, and your brain. The energy of your psyche resonates through your Third Eye. This area is also where you will experience your unconscious and conscious psychological tendencies. In Eastern philosophies, the Third Eye is the spiritual center of your brain that works with the rational part of your mind to deepen your insight.

When your Third Eye opens, you will be challenged to discriminate between your thoughts motivated by illusion, fear, and strength. You will need to learn how to develop your impersonal mind and remove yourself from mental and physical illusions that cloud your perception of reality. You will have the ability to know your soul from deep within honestly and to overcome your fears, worries, and thoughts. Your Third Eye carries the personal combination of your unique experiences and concerns and facts that are continuously active within your mental body.

The basis of the Third Eye Chakra is truth. It wants to get to the heart of what is proper to decipher those thoughts from what you believe is right. Many of the facts that people hold are nothing more than the remnants of a negative memory from the past. Someone who has been told that they are ugly or fat will perceive themselves as ugly or fat, whether real or not. This belief is burned into their brain from mental conditioning. Opening the Third Eye will help you to rid yourself of such preconceived notions as this.

As the foundation of wisdom, the Third Eye wants to break down stereotypes and help you see past any preconceived notions you have developed. You will also gain detachment from societal realities and see beyond the illusions that the world at large will feed you. You will learn the ability to think freely when your freedom is able to go beyond the realms of the realistic. Nothing is holding you back besides the power that your mind holds over you. If you can regain control of your mind and your thoughts, you will rise above any limitations you have set for yourself.

A healthy and balanced Third Eye Chakra will make you realize that no one social group or individual can determine the path you will walk in life. The change will happen, and a larger karmic entity's dynamic will drive that change. This change will ignite a chain of events that will move you along the path towards your life's next stage. You might now think that other people's opinions have the power to manipulate you into doing things you aren't prepared or ready to do. But that idea is just an illusion that will hold you captive in a situation that you don't want to be in simply because you are not ready to make a change. You will rely on the opinions of others to tell you how to live your life.

It is essential for you to live your life on earth to your fullest and then to leave quietly when your Third Eye is open. Death is no longer something to fear. Rather, it is the doorway leading you to the continuing lesson of your existence. People are perfect when born, and they can leave this world as perfect beings. You create karmic manifestations in your life that cause you to feel pain or suffer from the disease. Your conscious mind can detach from affliction and evolve into the ability not to endure pain. Then the spirit can release from the body at the end of its time. This choice is available to anyone who wants it.

Correspondences of the Third Eye

Correspondences are items that go along with other items to create an effect that is either beneficial or harmful. Each of the chakras has certain things that correspond with them to help them be healthy and functional. These items come from many different areas. The medicinal benefits of various herbs have been recorded for centuries. Herbs provide powerful ingredients that, if used properly, can help heal your body. Your body's natural healing process will utilize the ingredients provided by nature with fresh herbs for its benefit. The fresh bark, leaves, and roots of herbs are best used in their natural form. Herbs are also used in dried form or used as tablets, tinctures, capsules, creams, lotions, essential oils, powders, and salves. The vibrational frequency of herbs is in tune with that of our bodies. The Third Eye's favorite herbs are lavender, juniper berry, chamomile, thyme, frankincense, tea tree, and eucalyptus.

Aromatherapy involves using naturally distilled essences made from flowers and herbs to improve the health of your body, spirit, mind, and emotions. Plant essences become essential oils, and they can restore harmony and balance to your body and improve your life. Essential oils made of fruit, herbs, and flower essences are concocted to center your body and mind and enhance your life. They work as preventative measures and are an effective cure for many illnesses. Scents can induce tremendous power as they influence your moods. The most direct path to your emotions is your sense of smell. This influence is the principle behind the ancient art of aromatherapy. The same herbs that you will use for herbal Third Eye therapy are used for aromatherapy.

Colors are also used as correspondences. You can wear clothing or wrap yourself in blankets and shawls of the color that corresponds to a particular chakra. You can imagine that you are bathed in a light of that color associated with your chakra during meditation. The Third Eye prefers the color indigo, a deep midnight blue that is a combination of violet and deep blue, and carries both colors' attributes. One power of the color indigo is service to humanity and empathy for all beings. Indigo is powerful and dignified, and it conveys deep integrity and sincerity. The color meaning of indigo reflects excellent devotion, wisdom, and justice, along with fairness and impartiality. It will defend people's rights to the end. Indigo stimulates the right side of your brain to enhance creative activity and assist with spatial skills. It is a dramatic hue.

As the sixth internal chakra, your Third Eye governs your sixth sense. When it is blocked, you may feel disoriented, which will cause you a lot of psychic and psychological stress. You will feel lost and confused in an endless stream of information and nonsensical vision. You might also start to indulge in too much fantasy and lose touch with reality. You can use healing crystals to unblock and heal this chakra. The best crystals for this purpose are amethyst, sodalite, unakite, clear quartz, Moldavite, clear quartz crystal, iolite, sapphire, and lapis lazuli.

Responsibilities of the Third Eye

The Third Eye controls different areas in your body, and the effect will show when the chakra itself is injured or blocked. The Third Eye Chakra correlates to your psychological skills, mental abilities, and how you evaluate attitudes and beliefs. Located between your eyes, this mind chakra is physically connected to your pineal gland, as well as your pituitary gland and your brain. It controls your psychological tendencies as well as holding the energy of your psyche.

People are often afraid to look within and see the flaws and faults they carry. Acknowledging your inner truth can be scary, and your reasoning might be faulty. You fear being criticized because of your inner darkness, what goes with it, and other people's opinions. Balancing this sixth chakra gives you spiritual awareness of knowing there is a time that is appropriate for all things in life. It gives you the ability to let go of old patterns of thought and embrace fresh new ones. Continuing to fear the unknown will deprive you of living life to the fullest. The health of your mind and body are directly affected by your thoughts and attitudes. Depression directly affects your immune system. Your body is not able to heal because it is listening to the negativity in your mind. Your healing process is hampered by negative emotions like anger, jealousy, bitterness, and resentment. Recovery needs the unity of your heart, mind, and body. An unhealthy Third Eye chakra brings on recurring depression, nightmares, headaches, sleep problems, and spiritual arrogance.

A structure the size of a green pea, your pineal gland is seated in the middle of your brain. Once a tool that was revered by seers and mystics, it's now mostly dormant. Whatever divine purpose it once had was lost with the passage of generations. The pineal gland helps to connect all the powers of the universe. Every culture throughout the world touts the significance of the pineal gland. When you develop the powers of your Third Eye and open the doorway to all things psychic, you will enjoy the powers of astral travel, controlled dreams, clairvoyance, and telepathy. You will realize your ability to communicate with the divine. When you learn to utilize the benefits of the pineal gland, the illusion of separation dissolves. Because the gland is inside your brain, but outside your mind, a paradox is formed, creating a loophole to escape the contradiction of your reality.

This chakra holds the ability to connect you to the universe and fill you with a power much more intense and mystical than anything you can know with your physical senses. With the opening of your Third Eye and the pineal gland it corresponds to, you will be able to achieve elevated powers that include psychic vision, and you will connect intimately with the Divine.

CHAPTER 2
Symptoms Of A Blocked Third Eye

Located in between your brows, the Third Eye chakra is responsible for how you perceive the world. The energy of your Third Eye chakra starts in-between your brows, just above the bridge of your nose. This chakra is responsible for linking your mind and the outer world, embodying your ability to see both the inner and outer worlds. You will experience clear thought and self-reflection.

Your Third Eye chakra is driven by reflection, knowledge, and intuition. It symbolizes your connection to insight and deep wisdom, allowing you access to the inner guidance that comes from deep within your being. This connection enables you to cut through illusion and access more profound truths. Your Third Eye gives you the gift of thoughtful living. It is the center of your intuition and wisdom. The energy of your Third Eye chakra starts in-between your brows, just above the bridge of your nose. This chakra is responsible for linking your mind and the outer world, embodying your ability to see both the inner and outer worlds. You will experience clear thought and self-reflection.

Your Third Eye chakra is driven by reflection, knowledge, and intuition. It symbolizes your connection to insight and deep wisdom, allowing you access to the inner guidance that comes from deep within your being. This connection enables you to cut through illusion and access more profound truths. Your Third Eye gives you the gift of thoughtful living in the present moment. Your intuition and wisdom gather in your Third Eye chakra, allowing you to open your mind to deeper understandings and expand your awareness. When this chakra is balanced, you possess the ability to reflect on your inner self and see the world and understand it.

Key Characteristics of the Third Eye Chakra
Logic & Creativity — you will possess the ability to integrate your imagination, creativity, and logical thinking.

Vision — this is the link between your conscious mind and the physical world. It enables you to internalize visions from the outer world and reflect on them within.

Self-Reflection — you will receive the ability to examine your motives and reflect on your actions without bias.

Wisdom — this center of wisdom and knowledge wills your mind to deeper understandings.

Intuition — your new abilities are instrumental in perceiving the subtle qualities of a new reality. You will open your mind to intuitive sensibility and inner perception.

Your chakra system distributes the flow of prana or energy throughout your subtle body. Stress, emotional upset, illness, or conflict can cause blockages or imbalance in your subtle body. The seven internal chakras are interconnected. A blockage or imbalance in one will affect the others, and an energy disruption like this can cause you to suffer in your mind, body, and spirit. A blocked Third Eye causes emotional and physical stress. Suppose you are developing a deeper understanding of your world and expanding your intuition. In that case, it is essential that you open and balance your Third Eye chakra.

Clear and intelligent perception comes from an open Third Eye. In between your eyebrows at the center of your forehead, the Third Eye holds the bridge between your emotional and mental perceptions of the world. Dynamic balance in the Third Eye gives you the ability to trust your intuition, see-through deception, and quickly cultivate self-reflection. When linked to extrasensory perception, this includes visually perceiving auras or spirit guides. A chakra can be blocked or suffer from over-activation of the energy within the chakras. A backup will create an aversion to allowing life to circulate through this chakra, whether that blockage is from stagnation or fear.

When this sixth chakra is blocked, telltale emotions that might flood your system include disregard for intuition or emotional intelligence, gullibility, having a closed mind, and becoming stuck in the rational thought process. Other emotions that may circulate include feeling unable to work well with emotions, mentally exhausted, quickly following propaganda, weak imagination, and a profoundly subconscious fear of the truth.

The overactive chakra is a gathering of energy within one energy center. This causes the entire chakra system to become imbalanced. This will display as a strong emotional attraction to specific Third Eye chakra characteristics. Drifting between reality and the imagination, suffering nightmares, and hallucinations, or living in a fantasy world are all emotional symptoms of an overactive Third Eye chakra. These include self-criticism, struggling to stay committed to prior commitments, trying to force a process, or paranoia.

There are definite symptoms that will tell you that your Third Eye is not healthy and needs more attention. Becoming obsessed with spiritual matters is another symptom. You might use spiritual teachings to suppress or avoid painful emotions or unresolved issues as an act of spiritual bypassing. You are not merely a physical body. You might feel lost with no sense of purpose or path in life. This can lead you to follow an undesirable idea or group that will give you a sense of meaningful purpose in your life.

Your overactive imagination might lead you down the wrong path. You spend too much time worrying and regretting it. You worry about your future and regret the things you did in the past. You imagine everything that might go wrong and spend too much time worrying about the imaginary negative things other people are saying about you. You might feel life is too frightening to consider if you do not take appropriate action immediately to fix your broken life. You become stuck in analyzing everything while you try to figure out where your life went astray. It is difficult to turn off the churn mode. You may find it difficult to be present in the moment, and you might develop sleep issues. Your emotions rise and fall as you succeed and fail. You experience frequent or chronic headaches, neurological disorders, sinus conditions, and disorders of the eyes or ears, diseases of the outer brain.

Your Third Eye is responsible for much of your physical health. This chakra is the energy center that governs the health of the neurological functions in your body. This will affect your body's ability to maintain proper metabolic functions, fight off infections, and sleep well. You might become sick frequently, develop problems with high blood pressure, or suffer from insomnia. If the Third Eye is completely blocked, you can also suffer from poor vision, sciatica, seizures, sinus issues, and migraines. Extreme cases of Third Eye problems can lead to blindness or stroke.

This sixth chakra is located in the middle of your forehead between your two physical eyes. This chakra is called your Third Eye because it is where you get your psychic vision from. This is your vision to see into the astral realm beyond the physical world. Your dreams will become a reality in the vision of your Third Eye. Some intuitives can see angels, spirit guides, ascended masters, and people that have crossed over. Your Third Eye is how you can see these things. When you activate this chakra, you can see beyond what you can see with your physical eyes. This allows you to open your consciousness to deeper understandings that expand your intuition. When this chakra is balanced, you possess the ability to reflect on your inner self and see the world and understand it.

CHAPTER 3
Benefits Of A Healthy Third Eye

Many people are already familiar with their Third Eye chakra. While your two normal physical eyes allow you to see the physical world all around you, the Third Eye is associated with the future, intuition, and in some matters, with the spirit world as well. While everyone possesses the Third Eye, everyone has not taken the effort to open it and perceive the world. Those who do will find it offers them several benefits in their daily lives.

Because this sixth chakra resides at the highest place in the body, it holds a particular position and power class. Once you open up your Third Eye, it will bring your other chakras into closer alignment. This ability allows you to create an internal harmony that helps you face the world as a whole entity and not someone out-of-step with themselves.

Unaligned energies will disrupt your sleep just as much as a physical problem will. Because your Third Eye chakra aligns with your brain, and more importantly, with your pineal gland, it greatly influences your sleep quality. This allows you to see your dreams more clearly and ensures a better quality of sleep. Your dreams are most easily interpreted through the lens of this particular chakra.

The Third Eye helps you see the world outside yourself, and it enables you to see into yourself and the world present inside your mind. With a strong Third Eye, you will be in touch with your inner creativity in methods that might have been difficult or sporadic in the past. Your imagination flows through this chakra, and keeping it open will allow you to tap into that part of yourself with greater ease than you've ever experienced before.

Opening your Third Eye will also bring you in-line with the flow of the universal energies all around you. You will join the flow, rather than the rocks trying to break up that flow. People and events will flow toward you. Opening your Third Eye makes you a magnet; other people will be drawn to you, even if they may not quite understand why.

Everyone has times where they feel stressed about something. Maybe it was those bills you had come that you weren't sure you could cover or a conversation with a loved one about a complicated topic. You may feel frustrated with your work, your family, or some other part of your life. Stress weighs on you, clouding your mind and making it difficult for you to see the solutions right in front of you. Opening your Third Eye will pierce the fog of frustration and anxiety, allowing you to see past beyond previously impossible problems. This clarity of mind will put doubts to rest and enable you to see solutions that you would never have seen with the chakra closed.

One of life's eternal struggles is trying to figure out where to go from where you are. Everyone has a destination, and no answer will work for everyone. However, by opening your Third Eye, you will see yourself and find your path. By visiting the hidden world around you, and the secret world within yourself, you will understand yourself, your needs, and your desires more thoroughly than you did before. This clarity will allow you to find the drive you need to achieve success.

If you know you are dreaming, but you can't wake up, and you can't change the course of what was happening, you are having a lucid dream. Some people can take control of their goals and maintain their agency during these nocturnal adventures. Lucid dreaming is easy for those who are in-tune with this chakra. Opening your Third Eye chakra is the key to astral travel and projection. Connecting your mind to the greater universe around you allows your spirit to leave your body and experience other astral planes.

An open Third Eye will make you more in-tune with yourself and with the universe around you. You will shed stress and find the solutions you need in your life. Achieving that goal requires effort, but once you finally manage to scale that summit, you will know the worth of your effort.

CHAPTER 4
Methods For Opening Your Third Eye

Energy radiates from everything in the universe. Energy flows around, through, and into all things large and small in the universe. Your cells give off power in various ways. The different sections in your body emit different types of energy that will depend on what their function is and where they are located. Several other channels are located in specific areas of the body that allow energy to flow out and at a constant pace. These are your chakras.

Your chakras spin to move energy out of your body and counterclockwise to pull fuel into your body. The individual chakra's current state will determine the order that the power will flow through your body. The opening and closing of the chakras are part of your body's internal defense mechanism. If you have a negative experience, then the chakra associated with that feeling will close so that it can block out that negative energy. You can close off a chakra by holding on to specific thoughts and feelings, which will cause the chakra to close to protect itself. When you fix your chakras and open them again, the energy is once again able to flow freely, and your energy levels will soon return to normal. Since every chakra is attached to a specific part of the nervous system and the endocrine system in your body, a closed chakra could lead to an energy deficiency that might cause a severe physical ailment if left for too long.

All of your chakras are equally important to your body in terms of balancing and flowing energy levels. An ideal situation is when all seven of your internal chakras are balanced, open, healed, and spinning at the proper frequency. Your body will find ways to move energy around. If one of your chakras is closed, the one next to it or its balancing chakra will work overtime to compensate for the deficiency. Your body wants a balance of energy, so it will find ways to make this happen. If one chakra is underperforming, it will cause another to overcompensate, and this will upset the natural balance of your chakras. You need to recognize when your chakras are imbalanced because over-performing is just as bad for your body as underperforming. Here is a list of the feelings you might experience when your Third Eye chakra is not healthy:

Underactive -- clinging to the past, closed off to new ideas, anxious, disconnected or distrustful of the inner voice, rigid in thinking, too reliant on authority, and fearful of the future

Overactive -- Lacking good judgment, unable to focus, out of touch with reality, prone to hallucinations

Physical Symptoms of Imbalance – Excessive nightmares, poor vision, headaches, seizures, and insomnia

Associated Organs and Endocrine Glands -- Eyes, brow, pituitary, the base of skull, biorhythms

This chakra is responsible for your intuition, thought, manifesting, perception, and reality. When this chakra has opened, a doorway to spiritual enlightenment is opened. When this chakra is balanced and clean, you will possess emotional balance, self-awareness, insight, strong intuition, and clarity. An unhealthy Third Eye will cause you to suffer from mood disorders, mental illnesses, paranoia, depression, anxiety, cynicism, and closed-mindedness. This chakra can quickly become damaged in childhood if you were raised in a close-minded family who taught you to be obedient and never question authority.

When this chakra is unhealthy, closed, or blocked, you will physically suffer from migraines, sinus problems, vision problems, and earaches. You will either be ungrounded and dreamy or opinionated and arrogant. You will be stubborn and find it difficult to be open-minded. You will find it challenging to like other people. You will indulge in superficial or trivial relationships because you will quickly dislike or distrust others. Your opinions of the world will be rigid and nearly impossible to change. Reality will not be clear to you, and you will have problems connecting to your soul or your deeper self. You might also be addicted to those things that make you feel pleasure like status, money, sex, shopping, drink, food, or relationships.

A balanced and open Third Eye Chakra will make it easier for you to be more objective in your opinions and less rigid in your beliefs. Your life will be more fluid and free-flowing, and this will allow you to be more spontaneous and creative. You will feel more compassion and wisdom, which will let you reach your mystical state of being much more quickly. This chakra might be a bit more difficult to heal since it involves a lot of soul growth.

It is essential to explore new points of view if you truly want to heal this chakra. This exploration will assist you in breaking the cycle of being close-minded and rigid in your beliefs. You will also be easily lost in delusion and fantasy if you are not grounded in reality. Try to work on being present in your everyday life and not allow your mind to wander off too far.

Get outside and enjoy some sunlight every day. This daily habit will help heal the Third Eye Chakra because it will help clear your mind. Use blue lotus, rosemary, passionflower, lavender, jasmine, basil, saffron, star anise, or mugwort herbs in cooking or as incense. These will also make delicious teas. Add to your diet more of the purple foods. The Third Eye Chakra enjoys purple potatoes, purple carrots, purple kale, purple cabbage, eggplant, raisins, figs, and blueberries, blackberries, dates, and prunes. Use Third Eye Chakra appropriate essential oils like vetiver, juniper, sandalwood, clary sage, frankincense, and patchouli. Amethyst, labradorite, kyanite, lapis lazuli, sapphire, and shungite crystal can be carried or worn. Work on your yoga poses, especially head-to-knee poses, child's pose, dolphin pose, and standing forward bend. Light a candle and set it three to four feet in front of you and stare at the flame. Keep your vision focused in a comfortable, natural way.

One of the reasons this chakra will be damaged is when you hold on to core beliefs that are limiting. Your core beliefs are the deep convictions you hold about you that make you feel self-loathing, insecurity, and fear. When you uncover those core beliefs that you keep hidden, you will open this chakra and keep it healthy. Try to be more self-aware, as this is a necessary skill that you need to develop. Keep a private journal of your deepest feelings and thoughts. Sit outside at midnight and stare at the full moon.

The main reason that your Third Eye Chakra becomes unhealthy or blocked is that you identify with the thoughts you think because you believe in them. Learn how to observe your thoughts without feeling they are the ultimate truth. Feelings and opinions do not have any meaning unless we give them meaning. And keep in mind that your dreams express your inner needs, fears, and desires. They are naturally rich in symbols that hold meaning for your life. You interpret your goals with the help of your Third Eye Chakra.

And always remember to tell yourself how well you are doing. Use positive affirmations as a guided meditation to heal and balance your Third Eye Chakra. Use phrases that begin with the words 'I see,' 'I trust,' or 'I create.'

Yoga for Opening the Third Eye

When it is open and awake, the Third Eye chakra causes a person to dream quite a bit, have a good sixth sense, and possess a fantastic intuition. But people who do not have an active Third Eye will allow other people to make decisions they should be making for themselves. They might be easily confused and rely on misleading information. An overactive Third Eye will cause a person to live in a world of dreams and imagination.

To awaken the Third Eye, sit with the legs crossed and the back straight and firm. Put the backs of the hands-on top of the knees with the index finger and the thumb touching gently, and the rest of the fingers relaxed. The eyes will be closed, and the concentration should be on the Third Eye chakra's health and how it will benefit your body and the mind. Clearly and softly speak the word "om." Think about how the Third Eye chakra can affect life and energy. Keep meditating until a clean, refreshed feeling comes over the body.

The pose to keep the Third Eye chakra opened and balanced will quickly open the mind to fresh thoughts and new learning when it is regularly practiced. It will assist in the development of instincts and the strengthening of intuition. The Third Eye chakra governs the remainder of the chakras' functions, so it is essential to keep it balanced.

Sit on the buttocks with the legs crossed. Lay the hands on the knees with the fingers facing up and the thumb and the index finger touch. Keep the spine straight and firm but not stiff. Balance your spine on top of the pelvis and do not lean either backward or forward. Exhale and let the shoulders relax, and then inhale and lift the spine. Relax the body with the eyes closed. Keep breathing slowly and rhythmically while holding the pose for at least a few minutes before releasing it.

Affirmations for Opening the Third Eye

Affirmations are beneficial when used to heal the chakras. Declarations will quite often have an immediate useful effect on a person's personal vibration and mood. The affirmation words are powerful enough to give energizing power to the spirit, soothing sufficient to heal the body, and direct sufficient to reprogram the mind.

Each chakra has its affirmations that can be spoken silently in mind or out loud. Use affirmations as statements to repeat affirmatively while feeling the positive emotion associated with that affirmation. Affirmations can be used daily and regularly or anytime when you think your chakras might need a bit of healing. Affirmations will only be effective if they are specific to the chakra, particular to the person, and phrased in the present tense. The words that correspond to the Third Eye chakra all deal with clarity of vision and thinking and enhanced creativity levels.

- I imagine
- I envision
- I see

The keywords for healing the Third Eye Chakra can be used in combination with other words as desired:

I imagine peace	I see clearly
I imagine freedom	I see possibilities
I imagine power	I envision power
I see potential	I envision potential
I imagine wealth	I imagine health
I have vision	I see far away
I imagine peace	I see beauty

These can also be used to complete longer affirmations as desired:

- I see my imagination open to all possibilities
- I envision my inner knowing accepting my psychic potential
- I see the light of my higher mind illuminating my life
- I expect a clear path toward my goals
- I imagine my mind filled with guidance and wisdom
- I know when things are going well in my world

- I imagine a healthy spirit, mind, and body
- I see beyond illusions to the truth of the matter
- I envision a bright and lively future filled with hope
- I picture my mind focused and clear
- I imagine my life going exactly the way it should
- I am imaginative and insightful
- I see great possibilities in my future life
- I envision a peaceful world well filled with joy and love
- I imagine the goodness in others and try to see it

Color for Opening the Third Eye

The chakras change with the changes in human emotion. Whatever color, they usually correspond to the human being's current physical, spiritual, and emotional state. There is a special connection between the state of the body and the colors of the chakras. The colors are fluid, and if the chakra is blocked, the energy can no longer flow through the body. This is because there is a distinct and intimate connection between the entire body and the body's components like the mind, the soul, and the spirit. The colors of the chakras invoke different emotions. When someone sees a rainbow, they envision a sense of calm after a storm. Other colors will invoke different feelings in the mind and the heart. Color is a universal language that is spoken by all people.

Indigo is the color of wisdom and deep knowledge. This color is most often associated with night and opening the door to the divine. Your senses are more awake at night and more open to receiving messages from other worlds. Indigo clarifies your sense organs – your ability to see, hear, and feel. The color indigo connects your mind to your Third Eye by creating a bridge that links your brain's two hemispheres together and links the span between life and death.

The energy of the indigo is the energy of significant change. This energy will become higher vibrations on the spiritual level. You will need to remain consciously connected to your friends and family, so you do not become disconnected from reality. The ease with which spiritual matters come to you now might leave you feeling ungrounded. You will begin to recognize patterns in your life. You will recall your past while you clearly see where you are going. Indigo physically relates to your pineal gland, your brain, nose, forehead, eyes, brow, the carotid nerve, and the pituitary gland. People who carry vital indigo energy wear a noticeable glow. Their eyes are bright and full of deep wisdom. This calming power brings healthy shifts that change and transform you.

Symbolic thinking gets its energy from indigo as it connects the material with the symbolic. The effortlessness of action associated with indigo means that you do not impose your own will or ego on the situation when you are in action. The action flows around you and through you, and your accomplishments will become effortless. Indigo is a color that brings calm and tranquility. You will know peace in your life. Since you are now connected spiritually with the divine, you will know that your life is going well and nothing will need to be changed.

Blocking this energy that comes from the color indigo and the Third Eye will lead to much physical impairment in your life. You might suffer from sadness and loneliness as well as depression, and you might also experience hallucinations and delusions. Your Third Eye chakra enhances and develops your consciousness. The workings of the Divine are apparent to you as you become one with the Universe.

This ability is available to everyone, whether you know it as your sixth sense, intuition, your inner voice, or your gut feelings. The process cannot be forced or stopped. It is always there. Listen to the feelings coming from your subconscious mind. That voice from within is stilled too often by the demands of an energetic world. But your intuition is always there, and you can access it at any time.

Your intuition gives you that strong feeling that something might be wrong, so do not dismiss it because you can't rationalize it, or you may regret it later. Use the color indigo to help you connect with your intuition. It will connect with the deepest parts of you, allowing you to access your instinct, gut feelings, or the sixth sense.

CHAPTER 5
The Third Eye Doorway To The Psychic World

Psychics are nothing more than individuals who possess abilities that go beyond the boundaries of the physical world. They can taste, sense, feel, hear, see, or have the power of intuition. The basic definition of psychic skills is processing data from intangible and tangible stimuli on a profoundly spiritual, physical, or emotional level. This explanation is a broad definition because psychic abilities vary significantly in application and intensity.

Most psychic abilities are initially developed in childhood. Children feel more, hear more, see more, and notice more. Children are naturally more psychic because, to them, everything is real, including spirits. They don't know that you shouldn't believe in things like that, so it is natural to think for them. As children grow older and are steered more in math and science and less in imagination and creativity, they lose their psychic abilities. As adults, they accept that the physical world is the only realm that exists. But your psychic skills are never truly lost, just buried, and you can quickly resume them with a bit of practice.

Psychic Readings with Mediums

A psychic reading is a particular attempt by someone to find out information through the discerning use of heightened mental abilities. It can also be determined by using your basic human senses of sight, smell, taste, sound, and touch. These are a form of prophecy—different types of psychic readings that can be done. The reading may or may not involve the use of tools, and the psychic who is doing the reading may possess more than one area of expertise. These readings include astrological readings, reading the aura, psychometry, palm reading, and reading tarot cards.

- Reading tarot cards does not explicitly require psychic abilities. It can be used as a psychic reading tool for cold readings.
- Runes are the letters of the alphabet that are cast onto a table and then read to try to see what path a problem will take or to see the course of future events in someone's life.
- Psychometry is a type of psychic reading where the reader will collect details about someone from touching one of their possessions. The reader will usually ask for an item

that is a favorite one of the person they need information on, believing that a favorite control will hold more of their energy.
- Palm reading involves foretelling someone's future by reading the curves, wrinkles, shapes, and lines on a person's palm. This gift does not require any psychic ability, but previous knowledge of the subject is needed.
- The ancient study of numbers and their effect on the lives of humans is numerology. It is a reading based on the values of the numbers in someone's birth date or the numbers corresponding to the letters in their names.
- Lithomancy involves reading the signs shown by stones or gems that are dampened and then tossed out to land in a pattern.
- Distant readings include any reading done from a distance, without any contact between the reader and the subject, and can be done by telephone, mail, email, or any number of communication methods.
- Crystallomancy uses a crystal ball to do readings for people, see the past for them, or perhaps know future events for them.
- Cleromancy uses different variations, but they all involve casting out a group of small objects and reading the message that is evident in their proximity to each other and their orientation and position in the group.
- Aura reading involves seeing and interpreting a person's aura based on its strength and pattern of colors.
- Astrology studies the relative position and movements of objects in the sky to determine terrestrial events and human affairs.

A medium is a person who performs the psychic reading and speaks to those in other worlds to collect information for those in the current physical plane. They receive messages from the spirit world in many different ways. Words and images are sometimes accepted as intuitive information through mental impressions. These images are then relayed to the living which seeks information. The medium might even hear auditory messages. Those who have passed on before are full of useful information that they like to impart to the living, and they use the services of mediums to bring that information to those who want or need it.

If a medium is conducting a séance, they will relay messages from the dead through their voices as they slip into a trance and allow the deceased person to take over temporarily.

Relaxation, Emptiness, and Meditation

Emptiness is just another way to look at experience, a way to perceive things. The raw data of mental and physical events will not be added to or subtracted by emptiness. It allows you to look at the events in the senses and the mind without wondering if there is something behind them. This thinking method is called emptiness because it is void of all of the suppositions that people usually add to events to make sense of them. It helps to make sense of the world we live in and the events around us. People create stories to fashion the view of the world as they see it. These views and actions do have their uses, but they also have downfalls. They can pull attention away from the reality of the world and our place in it. These stories and views that are created as explanations can interfere with understanding the world and solving its problems.

For example, imagine that you are meditating and suddenly remember the anger you feel toward a specific person. You will immediately identify this anger as belonging to yourself or say that you have angry feelings. You will then elaborate on this feeling to be worked into your general views of that person or your memories of every time they made you angry. The problem with this method is that all of these stories and viewpoints are full of anger and suffering. The more you involve yourself in these stories and feelings, the further you will move away from the offense's source and learn the actual cause. So you are unable to find the start of the problem, solve it, and move on.

When you choose to adopt the emptiness mode, you will neither react to the anger nor act upon it. Instead, you will merely view the offense as part of a series of events. You will see that anger itself has nothing to identify with and is not something to possess. When you can master the mode of emptiness, you will remove yourself from the emotion and go to the source. This removal allows you to isolate the event that caused the feeling to find a solution to the problem. This solution will enable you to see the truth in events, whether large or small. In this sense, all things are empty since they do not have the power to create a reaction in you. You will see the labels like 'my anger' and 'I am angry' do nothing but cause pain and stress because they are unnecessary and inappropriate.

Emptiness will require patience and practice to master. It involves training in discernment, concentration, and virtue. If you do not receive this training, your mind will remain in the mode that continues to create views and stories of the world. The idea is to focus on the quality of the intentions and perceptions present in your mind so that you can process them and move them into emptiness. Once the events are there, you will be able to lose all of your attachments to assumptions, stories, and views. Your mind will be empty of delusion, anger, and greed, and that will make it devoid of stress and suffering.

This emptiness of the mind will bring you to true wisdom, which is the true nature of the mind and not something you develop or acquire. To achieve this, many followers of Buddha practice Mahamudra meditation. This practice is an ancient tradition of wisdom that started in India. The philosophy aims to communicate the real nature of the mind, and the meditation part of the practice will bring that knowledge and experience rapidly. The tradition is best known for its simplicity. The idea behind this method is to be aware, relaxed, and genuine in all situations in life to appreciate and accept the person you are. You will not need to change your current style of energy to achieve this level of mind emptiness. This experience will point you in the direction of the mind's true nature and help you be completely joyful and free.

When you begin the Mahamudra meditation, you will need to realize that the mind's true nature is to be aware, luminous, and empty. You also need to understand that confusion will develop if you do not accept that nature. And you will also need to know that all the mind's experiences and expressions are naturally luminous and empty, free of any fixation or negativity. You will use the meditation to bring your mind to a complete realization of these truths.

To begin the practice of Mahamudra, you will first need to understand what Mahamudra meditation is. Then you will use that knowledge to do your way so that it will become your own experience. You can't use willpower, luck, or accident to realize the real nature of your mind. This knowledge is where Mahamudra meditation is needed. There are three distinct parts to Mahamudra meditation. The first part is a view of your world's basic reality and mind, and it is known as ground Mahamudra. The second part, path Mahamudra, is where you will learn and begin to use the practice of meditation. Then fruition Mahamudra will show you what the path of this meditation will lead you to. When all three parts are completed, you will have a total picture of the awakening journey known as Mahamudra.

When you can look inside with a steady and clear focus, you will see that your mind is open, spacious, and transparent. Your emotions and thoughts will be vivid, but you will not be able to see them, as they will disappear the moment you focus on them. When you realize the spaciousness of your own experiences, you will experience the emptiness part of the wisdom of emptiness. But your mind will not be full of only emptiness. Your mind will also hold the wisdom part of the emptiness wisdom, and this will make your mind awake and aware. The understanding of emptiness will bring you true enlightenment.

Mahamudra meditation is the process of being familiar with your mind as it exists now so that you can learn how to relax within it. When you first look into your mind, you will find that it is very poorly organized and usually wanders in all directions. Your first task will be to bring clarity and order to your mind. Your awareness will naturally become sharper and more precise when you are more mindful of how your thoughts work. Ultimately you will be able to inhabit an exact dimension of openness and presence as your mind expands and relaxes. The Mahamudra tradition's meditation will teach you how to see clearly and rest like your mind. Most people think that you need to concentrate on something to meditate, focus on one thing, and concentrate on it. Mahamudra meditation is not like that, but it is more about allowing your mind to relax and be transparent in its state. The best way to think of this is to plan to be mindful while relaxing and letting go of stress. It may feel stressful and unnatural at first, but it will be an easy way to meditate with time and practice.

Sit down somewhere that you are comfortable and where you will be free from distractions. Pay attention to how the seat feels under you and how your body feels in the center. Feel your soft breathing and the thoughts in your mind. Sit quietly and breathe for a few minutes, taking as long as you need to rid your mind of your thoughts. Look at the space directly in front of you with eyes aware of what they are seeing. Spend a few moments resting at this moment. Make your gaze like the space in front of you; nothing particular to focus on while you focus on the area. If any perceptions, emotions, or thoughts come to your mind, you should accept them without comment or judgment. Whether the thoughts and feelings are bad or good has no bearing on the situation. Just let your mind rest where it is.

The object of this meditation is to not focus on any one thing. Instead, you will focus on the awareness, clarity, and emptiness of your mind, for this will bring you to the true nature of your mind. While you are thinking about the void in your mind, think about the openness and space within. The radiance of the emptiness will bring clarity to your mind. Keep sitting there and staring into space until you begin to feel calm and rested. Then spend some time thinking about the clarity of your mind. Since all of your emotions and thoughts are your mind's natural expressions, then take the time to see them but do not feel them. If an angry idea pops into your mind, then acknowledge the thought but do not allow yourself to feel the anger. What you think about does not matter, but the way you think about it does matter. This feeling is the awareness of the mind.

Now rest your mind for a few minutes and let go of all thoughts and feelings. Stare into space before you while you bring your mind back into the present. Relax and feel the awareness of your mind as it sits in emptiness. Relax in this space for a few minutes before resuming your normal activities.

Psychic Sense with Automatic Writing

Automatic writing is the act of writing words when you are in an altered mental state like a trance when this state comes from somewhere outside of your conscious awareness, like the astral plane. Spiritualists and psychologists have differing opinions about how automatic writing happens. Some people believe that it is messages from angels and spirits, and others believe that it is merely the work of the person's unconscious mind. A third belief is that automatic writing emanates from the individual's subconscious mind, acting as a doorway to their Higher Self or their soul. You will reap many benefits from automatic writing when you take the time to perfect your abilities.

- You will better trust your intuition and instincts
- You will feel deeply understood and supported
- You might contact your spirit guides and know their opinions and perspectives
- Your intuition will be better developed and sharpened
- Your ability to make smart decisions will improve
- Your daily life will be more clear and concise
- You will better receive guidance directly from your higher power

And besides all of these benefits, automatic writing is a calming practice that will metaphorically and open your mind. Automatic writing is simple in its execution.

- Be ready with a way to write responses
- Ask a question you need an answer for
- Write the question down or type it out
- Allow your body and mind to relax
- Let the writing flow freely

Writing automatically does not take the time to stop and proofread or add punctuation where it is needed. Just write. So what you write may not be grammatically correct or even make sense in some parts, but write what your soul is thinking and feeling. Developing this ability will most likely not happen overnight. It will take some time and effort, so do not be discouraged and try to be patient.

The first time you attempt automatic writing, you might easily find that it comes to you and the words flow freely. And then you might discover that the second and subsequent attempts do not flow as easily. This momentary failure is a perfectly normal phenomenon. Whenever people try something new, they generally approach it with a clear, open mind without any expectations. Then they begin to build up mental baggage that gets in the way of their spontaneous revelation. If this happens to you, approach it again with a clear mind, without expectations, and you will most likely succeed. Follow the steps for automatic writing, and you will soon be an expert.

Think of something that you need help with. Especially if you struggle to hear your soul's thoughts in your daily life, automatic writing might be just the vehicle you need. Begin each new session with a clear mind, meditating first to relax if needed. Decide what you want an answer to at that moment, some burning question that is tearing you up inside and you need help with. You will get a better response if your item is charged with emotion. Address your question to a specific entity, such as your unconscious mind, soul, or spirit guide. Keep your question as simple as possible because that will make it easier for you to receive an answer. And if you have more than one question that needs answering, do more than one session.

Relax your mind before you begin. This relaxation is one of the most challenging steps for people today because life is hectic nowadays. But it is probably the most crucial step because you will not be able to be receptive to messages from your spirit guide if your mind is clouded. Your writing will come to you much more comfortable when your mind is empty of thoughts and still and calm. Clear your mind with the method that works best. Some possibilities you can use are yoga, visualization, mindfulness, deep breathing, and meditation.

Allow yourself to enter a light trance. Humans possess the ability to enter a spell quite easily. Being in a trance is a type of altered consciousness where your brain relaxes its normal processes. The spontaneous flow of information will come to you in your automatic writing when your mind is relaxed. Suppose you need assistance to enter a trance state. In that case, you can try self-hypnosis, guided meditation, doing repetitive tasks, deep breathing exercises, repeating mantras as chants, or listening to music.

When the information begins to flow, do not stop it. As soon as you feel you are prepared, you can start to write. Your words might not make sense at first, but that is okay. If you can't understand what you are writing, that is a good sign because it means you are tapped into something that works far past your thinking mind. You might also be tempted to judge what you are writing but try not to. If you see that your thinking mind is trying to become involved, gently put it back into its relaxed state. You might need to repeat the exercise you used to get into the trance, which is normal, especially in the beginning. If you are not used to writing, that might take some getting used to, but it will come in time. And be sure to give yourself as much time as you need to be able to express the information that you need.

Don't try to interpret the information until you are finished writing. You will know when your session of writing is completed. You will abruptly stop writing, or your thoughts will begin to taper off gradually. Once you feel you are done for that session, it is time to analyze your writing. Look first for any coherent thoughts or sentences in the writing or any word you have often used. If you find your writing confusing, just put it aside and come back to it later. And if your writing makes absolutely no sense, then that might be a sign that you need to ask a different question.

The way you feel when you are writing is the best way to tell if you receive guidance from your soul. You may feel frantic and emotionally charged, or you may feel light and spacious. If your writing becomes heavy and desperate, it usually means that your writing is coming from your emotions or your mind. And review what you have written to determine where the words are coming from. Thoughts that come from your soul will always feel and sound clear even if the words you wrote are a bit garbled and nonsensical. Thoughts that are coming from your mind will often be vague, critical, or disjointed.

Psychic Power with Extrasensory Perception (ESP)

Extrasensory perception, also known as ESP, is the reception of information with the mind. This ability includes retrocognition, precognition, clairvoyance, psychometry, telepathy, and intuition. There is also the phenomenon of second sight, where a person can know things that are not readily available to the five senses, but they may receive a vision or otherwise see this information. ESP is the sixth sense of human beings. People often think that the activities that some call ESP are mere coincidence. You might think of a particular person, and then they come to visit.

Another example is when two people lock eyes simultaneously, as though each was thinking of looking at the other. The information traded in events involving ESP is felt in the heart, the soul, and the gut feeling that you often think. ESP is not held to any boundaries of space and time. It will allow you to see into the future, know the thoughts that others are thinking, and even manipulate physical objects. There are many different ways to experience ESP, but the most common ones for people to share are the six that follow.

Mediumship – This is a form of ESP that makes many people turn away. It involves communicating with dead people and channeling their spirits to receive messages for those waiting here on earth. Depending on the medium's intentions and the receiver of the message, this channeling can take the form of different types of ESP like clairvoyance.

Clairvoyance – This is the ability to see information about an event in the future, present, or past, including seeing things about a location, scene, person, or object by using only ESP. This power can happen unintentionally, but it is usually most vital when you are practicing meditation. There are different forms of prophecy. The ability to receive information through the human sense of taste without actually eating anything is clairgustance. If your sense of smell psychically brings you impressions of things, then you have clairvoyance. The ability to receive information through hearing using your sixth sense and psychic abilities is clairaudience. Clairsentience lets you feel the emotions and sensation that another person feels without being stimulated externally. This ability often goes along with paranormal activities, such as when you can feel the coldness emitted by a ghost.

Telekinesis (or psychokinesis) – This gives you the ability to directly and physically affect an object without ever touching it yourself. You will use only the energy of your mind and not any physical energy.

Retrocognition – This ability is the direct opposite of precognition. This ability gives you the power to see into the past, and usually into the distant past. You will be able to recognize events, places, and people from a past that you were never a part of. Another aspect of this kind of ESP is déjà vu, where you feel your recent experience was an experience you took part in before at some time in the past. People with this type of ESP are often able to furnish minute details of past places and people they should never have been able to see or know.

Precognition – This form of ESP is the ability to see directly into the future. If you possess this, then you will know information about scenes, events, places, and people before the experience even happens.

Telepathy – This is the ability that allows you to know what other people are thinking. If you have this ability, you can communicate with other people without speaking or writing words. You need no different sense to share besides the power of your mind.

The Eight Limbs of Mind Yoga

If you find yourself experiencing negative emotions or thoughts, that might be a sign that you need to grow, learn, and stretch emotionally. This experience is where mental yoga comes into play. Like in physical yoga, you might need to experience some discomfort to reach the place you want to be. Three ideas make up the practice of mental yoga. You will first need to accept that the emotions you feel are normal and a natural part of life on earth. You will feel regret, anger, sadness at different times in your life. If you accept these experiences and emotions instead of eliminating them or controlling them, you will feel better mentally. Use your innate sense of curiosity to learn from your adverse reactions while you view them without judging yourself or your responses. Your interest will engage your sense of logic. This reasoning will allow you to learn from your reactions and use that knowledge to intelligently create the next steps to lead you closer to your goals. And when your mind is finally free of the fight to stress about or resist your natural emotional states, then you will easily be able to commit to behaviors and actions that will help you achieve your desires.

Study the ancient texts that speak of the tradition of yoga. You will see that the actual physical poses are not the basis of traditional yoga practice. It is easy to think of yoga as a form of exercise for flexible people and like to do combinations of contortions. But the real gifts that yoga will give you will come from the spiritual, psychological, and mental aspects much more than the physical ones. Yoga is not an exercise but a way of life. Real yoga means treating your body and mind well all of the time, keeping your mental balance and physical balance, and keeping a healthy mindset.

The eight limbs of Ashtanga yoga will teach you much about the philosophy of yoga. These principles are the guidelines for living an enlightened life and are part of yoga's most authoritative and oldest teachings. The eight limbs deal with integrity, self-discipline, yoga poses, controlling your breathing, cultivating internal awareness, concentration, meditation, and transcending the self. You need to achieve the first seven if you want to achieve the eighth one. Begin by focusing on the first limb, where you learn to be moral and act all of the time ethically, not just when it is convenient. You will learn to practice restraint, refrain from coveting or stealing, practicing honesty, and avoiding violence.

Be gentle with yourself, even if it seems like selfishness. There is nothing wrong with putting your own needs first, at least some of the time. Indeed, you will not be able to take care of the needs of others properly if your own is not being met. When you are aware of your needs and confident and secure in yourself, you will bring more to the world. You need to learn to acknowledge your own needs, even if all you need is a break. Be honest with your feelings. This examination is the purpose of practicing mental yoga, learning to take care of you first in an elementary but non-selfish way. Mental yoga will benefit you in ways you might never have thought of.

You will be more prepared to deal with the issues you face daily. No one else can change you, and you are the only one who can control your behavior and actions. You need to own your peculiarities and not blame yourself for having them.

You will become more aware of qualities you might not have known that you possess. Using the dark and light powers in yoga will help you recognize those qualities you might not realize in yourself. You will become more mindful of yourself. Those random places in your body where you are holding little knots of energy, muscle tightness, or tension are the places where your emotional or psychological life has backed up and is stagnating. Like yoga poses to stretch your muscles and release physical tightness, mental yoga will release mental and emotional tightness. Practice working on your mind and soul to change yourself or accept that you can function well with faults and weaknesses.

Your romantic relationships will be so much more fulfilling. Living a life where you are more at peace with yourself and more relaxed will allow you to be the same way with your partner. You will be able to give away more love when you feel more love for yourself. You will be less reactive to small annoyances.

Your sense of self will significantly improve. Mental yoga will allow you to build a sense of trust in yourself. Physical yoga makes you want to exercise more and eat healthily. Mental yoga will make you more rooted in your sense of self. You will be more confident and mentally balanced. You will have energetic willpower and courage. You will have nothing to hide and nothing to prove.

Your level of anxiety will significantly diminish. Without mental yoga, you probably spend a great deal of time planning to fight or flee. With mental yoga, you will move from the more reactive state to the more relaxed state that will allow you to feel less anxiety. This relaxation will calm your nervous system and will enable you to feel more peace and love for yourself and others.

The more you can be confident in your gifts and grounded in yourself, the more you will resist the world's temptations to conform to society and its demands. You will know yourself and what you want and need, and you will not be afraid to pursue your dreams.

CHAPTER 6
Consciousness Of The Third Eye

Having an awareness of your mental and physical awareness is known as consciousness. Not all of the forms of understanding are the same. Besides the number of things that can affect these states of attention, you will find that all forms of awareness are the same. Like a stream of flowing water, the human being's consciousness is always flowing smoothly while it is continually changing.

The Third Eye States of Consciousness

Human consciousness can be altered in several ways. Anytime you question how the mind works, analyze a dream you had, or felt surprisingly energetic in the morning, you were relating your life to your consciousness. Some people wake up vigorous and ready to face the day, only to fall into a slump in the middle of the afternoon. Other people drag themselves through the day until the sun goes down, and then they are wide awake and ready for action. Circadian rhythms dictate the fluctuation of your energy levels throughout the day. These rhythms also play an essential part in your consciousness. Sometimes referred to as your internal clock, these rhythms' patterns will help determine your physiological states when you understand how the environmental and biological conditions will give you much information about how the circadian rhythms will affect your conscious states.

Sleep is a state of consciousness. For thousands of years, scholars, scientists, and researchers have been fascinated by sleep and its study. It has been theorized that there are several significant reasons why human beings sleep. Sleep is essential for the restoration and repair of your body. It will keep your mind functioning correctly in good health. It is also necessary for the restoration and revitalization of your physiological processes. Protein synthesis and cell division increase while you are asleep, which is even more evidence that humans need sleep to repair their minds and bodies. Your body needs defined periods of inactivity and activity to learn how to conserve energy. Humans also sleep to consolidate the information they have received while they are awake. Besides processing information obtained during the day, the brain will also take time to get ready for the next day. A lack of sleep will have a seriously detrimental effect on your ability to recall information. Another reason for rest is that it allows the brain to cleanse itself. During your normal daily activities, your brain releases waste products. During sleep, the brain's fluid level increases, and this fluid helps to wash out the waste products.

Another state of consciousness is the dream state that you will achieve while you are asleep. People dream of replaying the events of the day or of imagining what could be in their lives. And the brain spends a reasonable amount of time trying to make sense of the brain's activity while the body is asleep. There are specific characteristics that dreams will have. The emotions that you might experience in your dreams will often be acute, painful, and quite intense. A common thread in dreams is something terrifying, like being attacked or falling. Another common theme of dreams is finding yourself in an intensely embarrassing situation, like making a speech and finding yourself naked. If the emotion is strong enough, you might wake up in the middle of it in an attempt to escape the feelings. Sometimes your dreams are full of inconsistencies and ambiguities that can lead you to experience very bizarre dreams. One of the characteristics of plans is that they usually don't observe any laws regarding people, places, or time, and they often make no sense.

When you are dreaming, you accept the odd content of your dream without question. The strength of your perceptions and emotions feeds the unquestioning acceptance of the dream state. All of the events that happen within the dream seem to belong in the dream; even if they are out of place or illogical at the time, your mind will tell you that they belong in the dream. If you can recall the dream when you wake up, your logical awake mind will find the events strange and challenging to explain. And you will often experience strange feelings in your dreams. Some of the more common feelings are not being able to control your body, the inability to move, or the sudden feeling of falling.

During the dream, you will feel that your memory is more intense than usual, but when you awaken, you will often find that your memory of the dream fades rapidly as soon as you wake up. Some people are acutely unaware of dreams' characteristics and may not be aware of how common many of the traits are.

Your unconscious mind is a treasure trove of memories, urges, thoughts, and feelings that lie outside your conscious awareness. When you are unconscious, most of the feelings you have, like conflict, anxiety, and pain, will feel unpleasant or unacceptable while you are in that state. Your unconscious mind will continue to influence your experience and behavior, even when you are not aware of the influence. Think of the unconscious mind as looking like an iceberg. The small area that you see above the water level represents your conscious mind, and the large chunk that you can see below the surface of the water is your unconscious mind. Those things that are characterized by your conscious awareness are nothing more than the tip of the iceberg. The remainder of the information in your mind lies underneath the surface. And while this information might not be readily available to you consciously, it will influence your behavior. All of your basic urges and interests are contained in your unconscious mind. Your unconscious mind also holds the instincts that you have related to survival and those thoughts that are not usually socially acceptable, like aggression. You can use dream interpretation and free word association exercises to bring forth those ideas that are locking in your unconscious mind.

Third Eye Etheric Vision

The etheric body is the subtle body, the essence of the soul, or the aura of a person. This etheric body emits a low level of electricity known as an electromagnetic field. It surrounds the person in layers of colors that correspond to the different elements of your emotional, spiritual, mental, and physical health. People who can see these layers surrounding people have an etheric vision.

Before you can see an aura, you will need to be able to sense the atmosphere. An excellent way to begin developing your etheric vision is to pay attention to how you feel when you are around other people. Make a mental note of the gut reactions or physical sensations that you think. See if other people make you feel excited, calm, nervous, angry, or any other emotion you can think of. You might label that person with a color that you think fits them best. Someone sad might make you think of the color blue, while someone happy and upbeat might make you feel about the color yellow. As you become better at judging the other person's aura, identifying them with colors will be more comfortable.

Since the photosensitive cells in the sides of your eye are more robust than the ones in the center part of your eye, you will need to work on developing your peripheral vision. The photosensitive cells are a kind of neuron that mammals have in their retinas. They are especially sensitive to the presence or absence of light, so they are excellent receptors for a person's aura. Spend time paying attention to objects that are just outside of your direct line of sight. Don't cause yourself unnecessary anxiety while doing this by trying to strain or stress. Keep your breathing regular and take your time. As your peripheral vision becomes more assertive, you will see auras than you did before more easily.

The colors in a person's aura are among the most critical aspects of a person's aura. One of the best methods to employ for improving your ability to read the auras when you see them is to read and understand the colors in the aura. An easy way to practice this is to tape pieces of construction paper at different places in a neutrally colored and lit room. Then concentrate on the colors and the feelings that the colors of the paper give you. The most significant part of reading shades in an aura is knowing how those colors make you feel because, with the etheric vision, you will use all of your senses and not just your ability to see.

Now you are ready to begin practicing on people. Ask a trusted friend to help you and always get their permission first. Have your friend stand fifteen to twenty inches in front of you and in front of a neutral wall in color. Now stare at the wall and not your friend and see if you can sense their aura with your etheric vision. Now look at your friend gently, but do not stare, and use your telepathy to ask her aura to show its colors to you. Make a note of any colors that you see and anything else that comes to your vision. When you can see your friend's aura, ask them to move slightly to see if you can still detect their aura. Now do something to change their mood and see if the colors in the aura change.

Once you have mastered seeing the aura of your friend, then you should practice on yourself. Because your aura is always more challenging to see, this is one of the easiest ways to strengthen your etheric vision and your other psychic abilities. Start by relaxing in a quiet place. Clear your mind of any distractions. Before you begin, either think or say your intention to access and view your aura. Quickly rub your palms together to activate the energy between them. Keep doing this until you feel as though they are attracted to each other like two magnets. Now focus your attention between your palms and see if you can see the energy there. This is your aura. See if you can see the magnetic waves or any of the colors of your aura.

There are photographic methods that will enable you to see someone's aura, but that will not help you develop your etheric vision powers. Simply keep practicing until you are easily able to do it. Keep your attitude positive while practicing because any negative emotion will get in the way of your ability to see auras.

The Third Eye and Temporal Vision

The human field of vision is the area of space that a person can see simultaneously. It refers to the field of vision that you can see peripherally without moving your head or eyes. If an object near you emits light that you can see, then that object is considered in your field of vision. Temporal vision refers to the amount of time it takes you to see something instead of a spatial image, which is how much you will see in one glance. Temporal vision also refers to seeing things with your material eye instead of seeing things with your spiritual eye. Earthly vision will only come from the human eye and never from the Third Eye.

Another critical component for temporal vision is that it pays attention to time, logic, and sequence. While you are developing your spiritual eye, you will need to use your earthly imagination. You will need to practice seeing things in real-time before seeing and feeling them spiritually. You have the sensors you need to develop this method of seeing. When you link your Third Eye with your visual cortex, you will see with your heart and your mind.

Your physical eyes are useless for those times you need to see the invisible world's energy and spirit. Your retinas will only register a thin band in the energy of the electromagnetic spectrum. Physical eyes do not see infrared light or ultraviolet light, and these are two of the bands that your skin readily responds to. Imagine the optic nerve as the cable that transmits images to the screening room in the back of your head. It is not able to discern electromagnetic fields. Your visual cortex can translate energy into live images. The ability to see power is already in place in your brain. If you want to see the images you were always meant to see, you will need to let your visual cortex take control and change the signal's source.

Third Eye Spirituality and Mysticism

As concepts mysticism and spirituality have always been slightly difficult to define since so much of their understanding will depend on your perspective. All of the significant religions feature some form of mysticism, which has long been regarded as how you will reach the inner dimensions of your life, a place where you will achieve unity with the Divine Being of your choice. Spirituality is a concept with more possible meanings. Sometimes it is associated with those religious traditions that emphasize the growth of your inner life. This spirituality will include the ability to develop a spiritual experience that is deeper and more meaningful. In recent years the development of spirituality has moved farther away from the religious aspect and more toward the idea of achieving virtuous and ethical behavior as being normal.

As part of everyday life, mysticism is performing activities based on faith as you complete your regular daily activities. It is the search for and the pursuit of a relationship with a higher being. The desire is that this relationship will bring spiritual truth to your reality. Someone who helps you to achieve this religious experience is known as a mystic. The differences in psychological, social, and religious traditions will express how this term is defined. The mystic will also help you describe the communion that you were able to achieve with your Higher Power. Beliefs like these are considered to be somewhere beyond the intellectual or perceptual mind. Mysticism is spiritual, but it is not spiritualism as it is now defined. Mysticism is more of an organic process that includes the perfect union with the love of your Higher Power. The exact definition of mysticism will depend on the religious tradition that is defining it.

While mysticism is generally thought of as having religious connotations, it is not reserved simply for the spiritual element. The ability to become a mystic is an inborn trait, and there are two possible paths that you can follow if you desire this position. You can perform different activities that will bring you closer to communion with your Higher Power. These activities include meditation, which is one of the best ways to open your reception to messages from the Divine. Some people experience voices or visions because mysticism has been thrust upon them after any unexplained or traumatic experience. The traumatic experience does not need to be something wrong because anything outside of your normal realm of daily activities can be traumatic to your system.

Spirituality is the solitary adventure that your soul will take as it seeks for truth and morality in your life. Spirituality has nothing to do with worldly interests. And while spirituality is a broad term, it becomes even more comprehensive when defined by the different groups that seek spirituality. New age followers, Native Americans, polytheists, monotheists, and many others seek spirituality and determine what spirituality is. In all groups, it will deal with developing the master of the body, which is the spirit.

You can't define spirituality for anyone besides yourself because it involves deeply personal, subjective experiences. It generally includes a feeling of being connected to a more extensive power than you personally, and it affects your search for meaning in your life. As a human experience, spirituality is universal. You might describe your spirituality as transcendent or even sacred if that is what it means to you personally. It will bring a deep sense of being alive and connected to something larger than you are.

While you might define spirituality in terms of your religious experience, the act of being spiritual is much larger than being religious. While the two concepts are not the same thing, they are not that different, and they can overlap in your life. Spirituality will lead you to seek a better path for your personal life, more meaning in your life, and a way to feel connected to others. Mysticism will lead you to seek truth in life, the difference between right and wrong, and a desire to follow certain rituals that will bring you closer to your goal. Both of these disciplines look for the awe in ethics, reflective thinking, mental and emotional comfort, and a belief in something that will watch over you and help you on your journey.

Third Eye Psychic Visions

The word clairvoyance comes from two French terms that mean a clear vision. A person who has the powers of prophecy is known as a clairvoyant. It is the ability to get information from a physical event, location, person, or object. There is also the ability for remote viewing, which is the ability to perceive current events that happen outside of the range of a person's normal perception; retrocognition, which is the ability to see events that occurred in the past; and precognition, which is the ability to predict or perceive events that have not yet happened. All people are born with extraordinary psychic abilities, and they will appear in different people in different manifestations. You will know that you are clairvoyant if you can do any or all of the following:

- If you can paint pictures using words and feelings, or if spoken or written words give you the ability to create an image in your mind

- If you have vivid dreams that you can still recall once you are awake, or if you have recurring dreams that mirror events in your life
- If you see things just out of your range of view, and when you look to check, there is nothing there
- If you have dreams or visions that tell about future events
- If you feel an unusual awareness of the area of your third eye or if the middle of your forehead starts tingling

When you are a child, your pineal gland is functional and fully operational, and it is much larger than it will be when you are an adult. As you age, your pineal gland shrinks due to a loss of spiritual awareness. You will need to give your third Eye attention and love if you want to keep your psychic abilities intact. If you regularly use your Third Eye, you will enjoy oneness with the Universe. The main focus of many spiritual practices in achieving this oneness is to increase your empathy for your fellow human beings. At the same time, you release your worries and dissolve inherent stress. There are signs that you can follow that will let you know when your Third Eye is coming open and beginning to function

- As your Third Eye starts to open and you become more aware of yourself and your abilities, you will see that you are more loving, forgiving, and calmer. These changes in your temperament will help you move away from the processed foods that impact your Third Eye's health.
- You will become more sensitive to light as your Third Eye begins to open. This sensitivity means that you are beginning to see the world in a new, brighter light. The hues of colors will also appear to you as more rich and vivid. Anything related to light and vision will be expanded and heightened.
- As you become more accustomed to the presence of your spiritual self, you will begin to enjoy the benefits of the new view you have of the world. Your spiritual powers and intuition will guide you to make life choices guaranteed to make you healthier.
- You might begin to feel different sensations in your forehead, like a growing feeling of pressure between your eyes. Do not let this feeling worry you because it is entirely natural. You might also feel warmth in your forehead.
- You might also begin to feel experiences of an increased ability to see events before they happen. You may feel nothing more than a slight tugging in your stomach. Let this

feeling guide you forward, and do not overlook it. You will have an easier time allowing this feeling to show you how you realize it is totally within your control.

- As your power grows more substantial, you will be able to see and know more than other people know. You will be able to spot untruths easily. Your thoughts will be clear and will flow easily.
- The final sign of the opening of your Third Eye is so subtle that many people never notice. Your sense of self will increase so that you feel you are part of the fabric that makes up the Universe and not just a mere human with dislike, likes, and interests. You will begin to achieve the life that you always wanted as you rely more on yourself due to your increased sense of self.

It can be confusing or even scary in the beginning if you are not prepared to deal with the signs of having an active Third Eye. During this time, your greatest asset will be calming activities and meditation that will allow you to have a deeper connection to your spiritual self. No matter what path you choose, these manifestations are there to help you and should not be feared.

The Tunnel of the Third Eye

Many people trying to open their Third Eye have reported strange sensations during different learnings they are doing. One of the most common is the vortex that people often see while they are meditating. This vortex is a perfectly normal phenomenon and nothing to worry about. Seeing this vortex is something to be desired. This vortex is the tunnel that will lead you to the places your Third Eye will show you. It holds power to transport you to other realms.

When your Third Eye is open, and the vortex appears to you, it will look something like a golden halo of bright light that has spinning effects whirling around it. The center of the vortex is the tunnel you want to see; the tunnel will help you on your travels. If you do not know the tunnel or the vortex right away, just be patient because some people require more time to see it than other people. Your goal is to enter the tunnel when it opens to you since it will be your passageway to the astral world. Since your goal is to find this vortex with your fully-opened Third Eye, you can do things to make it happen.

- If you try to force the vortex to happen, it never will, so be patient and let it happen in its own time

- Follow your standard methods and plans for meditating, as long as these are working for you, and if you need to make changes, don't be afraid to do so
- Don't put your focus on the physical area of your Third Eye but try to focus on a point in the distance, something in the center of your vision, and set your concentration on this point
- Over time your consciousness will gradually increase, and your focus will naturally be drawn to this point, but let it happen in due course and never try to force the sensation
- Meditating to open your Third Eye and enter the tunnel is just like any other practice of meditation; it takes time and technique, and will become more comfortable with time and practice

You might not be seeing the tunnel or even the vortex, but you may have begun seeing an array of colors while you are meditating. This image is an indication that you are beginning to open your Third Eye and taking positive steps toward spiritual awakening. The color you see while you are meditating will correspond with your chakras, the energy centers inside your body. If you see more or less of one particular color, this might be a sign that your body's area is ailing and needs assistance.

Telepathic Awareness

When you can receive feelings or thoughts over distances from another person, this is known as telepathy. Telepathic awareness grows with the deepening ability of the Third Eye. When you use telepathy, you will not use any of the five basic senses of smell, taste, touch, sound, and sight. People who already have a close relationship are much more likely to be able to use telepathy. One example of this is the bond between twins who always seem to know what the other one is thinking no matter how far apart they are physically. This kind of relationship can be acquired with anyone if the conditions are right.

Telepathy is inborn in everyone, but communicating this way will require a conscious effort on your part. Learning how to use telepathy prevents many people from being able to since they approach skepticism and a lack of awareness. Another significant factor in people rejecting the idea of telepathic communication is the general view of society. Simultaneously, some cultures will embrace telepathy, just as many will reject the idea as nonsense.

You will be better able to communicate telepathically if you are in a relaxed state. Meditation is one good way to learn to relax and open your mind. When you are in the proper condition, your body will relax, your mind will open, and your spirit will be receptive to sending and receiving others' messages. Continue working to strengthen your ability to communicate with others this way and never listen to those who try to prevent you from doing so. When you try to send a message to someone telepathically, try to use great detail to envision the other person. Imagine that they are standing in front of you and having a conversation with you. You will not get instant results, so be patient while you are learning.

While you are sending your message, you should begin to feel that your message is being received. When you think of this, you should stop trying to send your message. You might think that you imagine things when you first begin receiving messages from other people. Listen to these thoughts and remember them, but keep in mind that they are perfectly normal. You will receive communications in various ways. You will experience desires, images, thoughts, emotions, and feelings. Some people can even receive and send messages while they are asleep.

You will relate to people with greater understanding and on a higher level once you begin to connect with other people using telepathy. This ability will have a serious effect on your relationships. And communicating telepathically is a more efficient method of communication. It is instantaneous, free, environmentally friendly, and the location is not essential as telepathy works anywhere. You will easily contact anyone, anywhere, at any time. You will also block other people from sending messages to you if you do not want to communicate with them. This communication will take a bit more effort to learn, but it is well worth the effort.

CHAPTER 7
Astral Beings And The Third Eye

Your Third Eye is a light that you will see when your eyes are closed, visible there behind the darkness. Through the morning of your spiritual vision, you will be able to look into other realms. The Third Eye reflects cosmic energy as it enters your body and helps to sustain you. This cosmic energy enters you through your Third Eye.

You will see that the spiritual eye looks like a halo of golden light surrounding a circle of deep blue. Centered in the blue circle is a five-pointed, silvery-white star. If this symbol appears in your meditation, you should concentrate on the star in the blue field center. While you are focused, the golden halo will gradually expand and stretch into a tunnel. If you allow yourself to pass into the tunnel, you will be entering the light of the astral world. The blue light will form a tunnel that will lead you into cosmic consciousness. As you pass through the star in the center, you will then enter the astral world beyond creation.

Other Worlds

Parallel worlds do exist, and they are detectable because they interact with our world here on Earth. It isn't easy to test these other worlds' actual presence, but those who believe in them believe entirely. There is compelling evidence to verify the existence of these parallel worlds. One of these pieces of evidence comes from the world of quantum physics, which theorizes that every one of the possible outcomes of any situation does happen. Still, they occur in different Universes because only one result of a case can occur in each Universe. This would necessitate an infinite number of parallel worlds to allow this theory to be possible, and this idea is just as valid as any other explanation. As of now, no observations or experiments have wholly overridden the possibility. The second theory comes from the world of physics and the idea of the multiverse. While it is speculated that the Universe that we live in began with the Big Bang, it is also supposed that the Big Bang was not the beginning that we have always assumed that it was. The theory is that cosmological inflation happened before the Big Bang, and where the inflation ended, the Big Bang happened. This inflation did not end everywhere at once, so where it did not end, other Universes would have been created after our Universe was created.

And once inflation begins, it is impossible to stop it, and when inflation ends in a particular place, there will be a Big Bang that will create a new Universe.

While there is no concrete proof that parallel worlds exist, there is also no concrete proof that they don't exist. These other worlds can share the matter with our Universe. And there is evidence that shows that a parallel world is not only possible but also probable. Recent radio wave studies have demonstrated radio waves below the polar ice cap, in an area that should have been frozen since the beginning of time. This evidence goes right along with other astrophysical quandaries like black holes and pulsars.

Traveling the Astral Planes

Astral travel goes by many different terms, depending on the tradition or religion that is referring to it. The Hindu body of bliss, Tantric spiritual body, the Christian experience of other heavens, Taoist diamond body, Egyptian ka, Buddhist light body, energy body, dream body, or astral body can be known as the Hindu body of bliss. All these terms mean the same thing: astral travel. The human being's standard design includes the subtle body, and it is the subtle body that astrally projects and is active during lucid and unconscious dreaming. Out-of-body experiences are usually the combination of dreaming and astral projection. When the subtle body is cultivated, it will survive the physical body as a consciousness model. Part of the spiritual energy training paths for developing the subtle body is lucid dreaming and astral projection.

Out-of-body experiences can be involuntary or intentional. Depriving yourself of food or water, illness, or trauma can all trigger an out-of-body experience. Good opportunities for purposeful astral experiences are lucid dreams. The adventure begins with the knowledge of consciously observing the body after leaving it. Awareness can be directed to activities or locations of your choice with some lucidity and practice.

The subtle body or the astral body has long been acknowledged as truly existing. Esoteric techniques for healing were developed from the recognition of the celestial body. Distance healers, followers of the Reiki method, and energy healers are familiar with these techniques and use them in modern times, working specifically with the energetic body.

The rational soul and the physical body are linked together by an intermediate body of light known as the astral body. The middle world between Earth and Heaven is the astral plane. When your celestial body leaves your body to travel the astral plane, astral travel is known. Accounts of astral travel are widely documented. These travels are usually described as the journey of the soul into other realms.

People who practice astral projection validate the existence that there is life after your physical body's death. They describe the experience as finding themselves present and aware of themselves outside of their physical body. They can taste, smell, touch, hear, and see. You cannot dismiss the idea that your physical life is nothing more than a moment away from the spiritual plane of existence. A switch is activated inside of you when you are engaged in conscious astral projection, sleeping, or deep in meditation. This switch is also known as your pineal gland, which is necessary for opening your Third Eye, which helps bring you closer to the possibility of astral travel. Chemicals released from the pineal gland cause your soul to leave your body during near-death experiences, when your soul is leaving your body at the point of death, or when you are sleeping or meditating, and the soul goes for astral travel.

You have no control over what your soul does while you are sleeping because that is when your subconscious owns your soul. There are benefits to consciously practicing astral travel. It will take you beyond the limitations of the rational and the physical. Many people experience the inner blooming of their spiritual being and a profound shift in their astral senses. They enjoy a complete transformation of their perspective of themselves as physical and spiritual beings. After astral travel, these people use a greater consciousness during life activities because they are secure in knowing that they are more than just mere physical beings doomed to live short, boring lives.

There are many benefits to astral travel. It will enrich your soul and your life. You will have a better understanding of the spirit world and your place on the astral plane. Your religious limitations will shatter. Any restrictions you had previously put on your life and your beliefs will end when you begin astral travel.

Out of Body Experiences

The experience where your soul leaves your body is astral projection or out of body travel. Your soul is free of your physical body, and it can travel independently of your physical body. This travel is not the same experience when someone dies, and their soul leaves their body permanently. Astral travel allows your soul to leave you and roam free while you remain alive, and then your soul will rejoin your body. Astral travel is an old idea that is present in many cultures around the world. It will sometimes happen during meditation or while a person is dreaming.

Western thought says that the astral body is a form of light that links the soul to the body's physical part. The astral plane is composed of stars and lights, as it is the plane located between Earth and Heaven. The stars and planets of the astral plane are populated with spirits, demons, and angels. The celestial body, also known as the subtle body, and the planes of existence the subtle bodies are associated with, form an esoteric system of the cosmic phenomenon. These planes of reality and the heavenly bodies are often pictured as a series of circles winding around and over. A particular type of celestial body will travel to each realm.

In the Biblical world, the subtle body links to a psychic cord's physical body. It is taught that the silver cord should never be entirely loose from either the subtle body or the physical body. In ancient Egypt, the soul, the subtle body, has the power to hover over the physical body and watch it. In China, the Taoists believe that the two forms of the person, the subtle body and the physical body, can leave the other to perform different acts and then come back together later.

You can prepare your body for the practicing astral projection in various ways.

PREPARE FOR TRAVEL – Since it is often easier to reach the needed states of heightened awareness and relaxation in the early hours of the morning, you should begin then to prepare for astral travel. You can also do this at night, in the last moments before you lie down to go to sleep. Astral travel is a purely personal experience, so do what is best for you.

Since you will need to be in a state of complete relaxation, you should prepare while in a place that you feel comfortable. Lie down in your bed and relax your body and your mind. Astral travel is more comfortable to do when alone, so if you regularly sleep with someone else in the room, you might want to sleep in another room while you prepare. A time when you are alone is best so that no one could accidentally walk in and disturb your travels. Get rid of any noise that might distract you, and close the windows and the curtains to allow the room to be dark.

Lie on your back in whichever room you have chosen. Try to clear all distracting thoughts out of your mind as you close your eyes and relax. Your goal here is to attain a state of complete body and mind relaxation. Systematically flex your muscles and then let them rest. Begin with the toes and then work your way up to your head and neck. Make sure that every muscle is completely relaxed before you move on to the next one. Don't allow any tension to gather in your neck and shoulders, and breathe deeply and slowly.

Focus on your deep breathing. Try not to let outside thoughts and worries get into your mind. Also, don't become preoccupied with thoughts of astral travel. Right now, all you need to be concerned with is achieving a state of relaxation. If you have quartz crystals, you can use them to raise your vibrations and help them to move faster. Place the crystal on your forehead over your Third Eye and let your mind clear as you feel the vibrations grow from the crystal. The crystal can also rest on your abdomen or chest or hold it in your hand. It will protect you and empower you because it will give off high vibrations.

Release your soul from your body – Allow your mind and body to get close to sleep but don't fall completely asleep. You need to be in a hypnotic state for astral travel to happen, a place just at the thin line between sleep and awake. Keep your eyes closed and let your thoughts travel to one single part of your body. Focus all of your thoughts on that particular part of your body until you can see it correctly, even with your eyes closed. Let all other ideas fall away while you complete this exercise. Then try to flex that part of your body using only your mind and not your muscles. See your toes wiggling, or your fingers curling into a fist in your mind and keep picturing this until you feel as though these parts are moving. Now broaden the focus of your thoughts to include your entire body. Use only the power of your mind to move your head, arms, and legs. Keep focusing steadily on this technique until you can use just your mind to move your whole body.

Now you will probably feel a series of waves as your soul gets ready to leave your body. If you feel fear, your soul might hesitate, so try not to fear this part. Let the vibrations take over you as your soul prepares to depart on its astral travels. Continue to remain relaxed while you imagine the room that you are lying in. In your mind, move your body so that you can stand up. Once you are standing, look around the space where you are resting. Now keep using the powers of your mind to walk across the room and turn and look at your body lying on the bed. If you can feel that you are looking at yourself from across the room, then the out of body experience is successful. Your body and your conscious self are now separate entities. You might need a lot of practice to get to this point. Anyone can participate in astral travel if they desire and are willing to practice and have faith. If you are having trouble altogether leaving your body, just practice moving an arm or a leg until you have mastered it. And once you are done with your travels, you will return to your body. Let your soul sink back in, and then move your toes and fingers physically to help yourself fully awaken.

Complete your exploration – When you have finally gained the ability to leave your body, you will want to have some confirmation that you are really in two separate worlds at the same time. When you have been able to leave your body, turn to look at yourself, and then return to your body, you will try something different the next time. You will leave your body, but you will not turn around to look at yourself. You will leave the room that your body is lying in, and you will walk to another place in the house. Pick up an object in the other space, maybe an item that you never really paid any attention to in your physical self. Remember as many details of the object as possible, paying attention to its size, shape, and color. Now return to your body and wake yourself up. Get off the bed and walk into the other room and find the object you had before. See if the details are just the way you remember them from your travels.

Once you have mastered astral travel, make more changes on future trips. Try to go to new locations that are less familiar to you. Always make a note of details where you are, and try to remember things that you will verify when you are back in your physical body. After you do this a few times, you will be able to go to places that are unfamiliar to you and then return to those places with your physical body, and they will seem familiar to you. Astral travel is not dangerous. You might feel more secure, picturing a bright white light surrounding you while you travel, a light that will protect you from harm.

Dream Control

If you have ever started dreaming and then suddenly known that you were in a dream, then you had a lucid dream. You were also experiencing a lucid dream if you have taken control of the path that your plan was taking. Usually, when people dream, they have no idea that they are dreaming; they are just doing it. Some people can go into a dream and be completely aware that they are dreaming and in control. Lucid dreams have been recorded since the time of the ancient Greeks.

Like most of the dreams that you have, lucid dreams will happen during those periods of rapid eye movement type of sleep. It usually occurs spontaneously, although some people can train themselves to enter a lucid dream state. The ability of people to influence their dreams has a great deal of variation. Some people will wake up immediately, and some will continue with the dream. Some people can control the entire dream or certain parts of it. Lucid dreaming will allow you to explore the worlds inside your mind while fully aware that you are in a dream. It is an almost magical feeling.

Lucid dreaming may have different applications in the practical world. It can help people to lessen fears or phobias. If someone who has recurring nightmares can become lucid during that nightmare, they may be able to work through their fears. People with phobias can dream about the dread and then use it to control their worries. Therapies like this are possible because the dream state's environment is a safe place that you can quickly leave if the situation becomes too harsh. Lucid dreaming can also be used as entertainment because you can go anywhere you want while you are in the dream state.

There are techniques that you can use if you would like to become better at lucid dreaming. One of these techniques is called reality testing. This test involves a way to verify whether you dream both in the dream and real life. During different times of the day, look at your surroundings, and see how you react. Check your surroundings to see if you are awake or asleep. Set an alarm clock for every two to three hours during the day to make sure you are awake. During a dream, you can look into a mirror to see if you can see yourself. Try to push your hand through your other hand or a wall because you will not be able to if you are awake. See if your hands look familiar to you. Look at the clock on the wall. If you are awake, the time will seem to crawl. If you are in a dream, then the time will continuously change and fluctuate. Pinch your nose and see if you can still breathe.

Try to write down your dreams in a journal every morning as soon as you wake up. When you take the time to write down your dreams, you will be forced to recall the details, which can help you know more about your dream. It can also help you plan a particular dream for lucid dreaming because it is easier to take control when it is something you like or a familiar subject you dream about.

You might sometimes feel that you are trapped in a lucid dream with no way to escape, but there are methods for waking yourself up. If you yell while dreaming, it is a signal for your brain to wake up. Open your eyes and blink rapidly. Try to activate a different part of your mind by reading something in your dream. And if all else fails, go to sleep in your vision because this will disrupt the dream sequence.

CHAPTER 8
Spiritual Beings And The Third Eye

Having a Third Eye that is open and fully functional will enable you to see the entities that come from other astral planes and reside with you on Earth. The ability to see these beings depends on you being in tune with your psychic abilities. You will meet beings familiar to you, and some will seem unique. Receiving messages from people who have passed over, advice from your spiritual guides and deceased loved ones, and psychic information from the energy fields of other people is a part of daily life as a modern mystic.

While your physical eye will show you what is in the world around you, your Third Eye will open you to the possibilities in the astral world. While it is essential to have wide-open eyes to see things, a wide-open Third Eye will allow you to see life beyond life. It is a sense that sends and receives information. You will use your Third Eye to answer questions and understand hidden connections with other people. You will feel more powerful and more empathetic as the possibilities open up before you.

Beings currently walk the Earth disguised as humans, deliberately confusing and fooling you. You might never know who you are dealing with when it comes to a spirit. Any spirit you might encounter can be evil and ugly spiritually or kind and loving, but you may not know until you become close to them. The spirit form is invisible to most people, and you will only be able to see them in their human form.

Earthbound Spirits

Instead of going out of your area, as it should when it removes from the body, the nucleus of the spirit stays behind, trapped on earth, and the nucleus generates a spirit of its own. The energy of the spirit gathers to recreate the form of its lost human being, and it takes on the characteristics of a ghost. It will put aside the fact that it was once human and lives as a form of energy attached mostly to a place or object of former importance. Spirits that are bound to earth have no timeline and sense of time. They have no permanent human form, for they have no hunger or thirst. They will drift unattached until a living person comes along to give them someone to attach with.

An unattached spirit will become a ghostly being when it encounters the human it wants to attach with. Those people who are naturally more sensitive will attract more of these spirit entities. Not every soul will go toward the light at the moment of crossing over from life to death. Some passing souls either do not recognize the light, or they are afraid the light might not be genuine. The mind of the spirit may not trust the light. These spirits will cling to the people they know and love on earth, refusing to cross over at the moment of death. A person like you will come along and give the lost spirit a person to attach to, someone to make new adventures with. The entity the spirit attaches to will help the spirit to grow stronger. Your life force can feed the spiritual side of the ghost. Spirits use their force field to gather particles from electromagnetic fields. This enables them to appear to others, using colors, sounds, or aromas that attract the other entity.

Loved ones who have passed on will show themselves to loved ones by entering their immediate realm or appearing through dreams. When this happens, the spirit must invade the realm of reality, which will give off a gold or silver glow. The spirits will also use small creatures like birds or butterflies to appear to their loved ones left behind.

They might also turn the living person's attention to a particular song, create a coincidence, or waft a fragrance; they do something that stirs the memory of the living person. Other times they will activate a specific memory in the mind of the human they are trying to attract. They can even use a form of a hand to caress the skin of their loved ones. This is an act that takes an enormous amount of effort and focus on the part of the spirit. Still, to them, the possibility of making contact with a loved one is worth the effort.

Knowing your Spirit Guide

Everyone has a spirit guide, a being of light, ancestor, angel, or other entity whose one job is to surround you with love, supporting and guiding you on your journey through life. Your guide may have been with you before in another life. It might be a person you once knew or a loving ancestor determined to help you. You will always have a relationship with your guide as they are there to help you, but you have free will when communicating with your spirit guide. They will stand beside you silently, waiting as they cannot make actual contact with you unless you initiate the contact. This rule becomes voided if you find yourself in the middle of a life-threatening emergency. This information is vital for you to remember so that you do not think your spirit guide is not present with you at all times.

Your first step in making contact with your spirit guide is to have faith that they are with you because if you do not believe in them, you will never be able to communicate with them. And you will most likely have more than one spirit guide. Some of your companions have been with you since birth, and some came along when you needed exceptional help. If you need more spirit guides, you can request them to come to you. They will all work together because they have your best interest in mind. Your spirit guide team might include any or all of the following:

Ascended Masters were humans at one time, and many of them return to act as spirit guides. As leaders in the spirit world, as they were in the human world, they are now guiding your spiritual development and keeping you safe in the world.
Helper Angels are freelance angels who wander around searching for a human with a particular need or are in a specific situation where they need assistance.

Departed Loved Ones are those people you have known who have passed on but became your spirit guide. Any human being who has passed on can become a spirit guide, and they usually look for humans with interests similar to theirs or members of their own family. If you are a nurse, your departed loved one might be a former nurse as they will understand your feelings and frustrations.

Guardian Angels belong to you and only you because they have devoted all of their time to taking care of you. They usually come to you before you are born and stay with you until you die. You can reach out to your guardian angel at any time that you need help.

Spirit Animals are animals who have passed on and returned to assist humans on earth. Often, a pet that you once had will return to your life as your spirit animal, although it can be any animal that has something it needs to help you with at that time. They might be teaching lessons related to their living form so that a wolf might teach you about survival, and a fish might assist you with learning to swim.

Archangels are full of powerful energy, and they are the leaders in the world of spirit guides. Those who are sensitive to spirit energy or empathize with you will often feel a surge of power when you call on your archangel. Each of the archangels has one area of specialization.

Your spirit guide can't communicate with you until you communicate with them first, but they can send you little messages when they feel that you need a push in a particular direction. You might see a book on exotic travel on the very day you think you are at the end of your emotional rope. They will also communicate with you by using numbers or sequences of numbers. If your job interview address is a number that you consider to be a lucky number, then that is probably your spirit guide sending you a message. If you hear a song that is especially meaningful to you after a rough day at work, then your spirit guide is sending you a message. They might also send you a dream with an idea to solve a problem you have. There are ways that you can facilitate communication with your spirit guide.

Use some sort of tool for divination. There are many of these tools you can use like runes, tarot cards, and oracle cards. Before you use any of these, hold them in your hand, and ask your spirit guide to assist you. Use thoughts to send your spirit guide a message. You can have an idea or make a formal request or prayer; any communication method will reach your spirit guide. Develop some sort of spiritual practice that you do regularly. You can have a routine that you do daily, weekly, or monthly as long as you have a ritual of your own.

Work to improve your intuition. You will be able to improve your powers of clairvoyance with study and practice. Begin by practicing with small things that are relatively meaningless. You can try to think where a coworker will choose to go for lunch before inviting them out. Or dump a few of an item into a bowl, like mini marshmallows or marbles, and try to guess how many there are before you count them.

Spend some time studying the idea of the spirit guide. If you take the time to know what they are about, you will be easier to communicate with.
Surrender a problem to your spirit guide. If you have a question that you just can't solve, give it to your spirit guide and let them show you the way. Do this even if all you need is a little break from the events of life. Even surrendering the issue for a little while will give you a mental break, and the spirit guides will have an opportunity to send you some ideas.

Assign your spirit guides their name. Give them a name that is one of your favorites or one that is meaningful to you. It is easier to talk with someone when you know their name. This familiarity will make you more likely to connect with them regularly because it will make them seem more real to you. Start a journal to write about your spirit guide. You can also use this journal to write messages to your spirit guide to ask for their guidance and help. You can also keep a list of signs that they send to you. Watch for signs from your spirit guide. As you spend more time watching for alerts, you will be able to see them more often. And as you grow more alert to your spirit guides sending you signs, they will begin to send even more.

Try to be more present in the everyday. You need to be mentally present in your life if you want to know when your spirit guide sends you a message. People often miss notifications because they are too busy hurrying and don't see the message. Engage is a period of quiet reflection daily, even if it is only thirty minutes. Meditation is a proven method for clearing accumulated thoughts from your mind.

Earth Angel

Angels on earth are real heavenly angels who have been born into a human body so that they can carry out essential missions here on earth. Earth angels are here to open the hearts of others and show them the goodness of true love. They will work to protect people from further harming one another and to preserve the environment. They also want to raise the vibrancy of earth and humanity to communicate with each other and the spirit world more accessible

Earth angels are highly sensitive people who cannot tolerate any form of violence. Being guided by the Laws of the Universe that pertain to trust, purity, and love, they automatically expect that all people will feel the same way, which is why their hearts are often broken and their spirits crushed by the evils of the world. They do not remain sad for long, even though they will never understand the world's violent ways.

They will often look much younger than they are because their happy outlook on life keeps them young at heart. As children, they were frequently bullied or teased because of their different behavior and appearance. Earth angels are highly sensitive to changes in the earth's energy and the people around them. They see all people as good people, even with the shortcomings and imperfections that the Earth angels look past. People often take advantage of their excellent nature because of their kindness, which is often mistaken for weakness. But the Earth angel sees misfortune as a blessing in disguise because they are eternal optimists and never stop believing in people's good.

Many Earth Angels have a difficult childhood. They are often misunderstood by their family members and made to feel that their kindness and gentleness make them look weak. Thus, many Earth angels think that they do not fit in and do not belong here on earth. They may spend time staring up into the night sky and hoping to go home as soon as possible. All of the negative experiences they have might give them low self-esteem. They continuously apologize for things that are not their fault because they feel guilty about everything.

But even with all of the negativity in their lives, Earth angels have tremendous patience and are eternal optimists. They will stay in a relationship that most people would have given up on. The Earth angel needs to reach a total breaking point before they abandon anyone. They always have kind words and words of wisdom for everyone, which is good because everyone brings their problems directly to the Earth angel. They will ignore their own needs in favor of taking care of the needs of the world. But do not take the Earth angel out into a crowded place. They will not do well there because of all of the chaos and noise. Earth angels like solitude and peace.

Earth angles see peace, beauty, and love abundantly in nature. They view the world with awe and astonishment because the world is a beautiful place full of beauty. They are protective of the planet and nature. And no matter what form a life takes, the Earth angel will love everyone equally. They feel interconnected with the Universe and the world, a great oneness with everything and everyone. And no matter how old the Earth angel is, they will still believe in fairy tales and miracles. They have no fear of death because, for them, it means they are going home.

Divination

Many of the cultures around the world practice the same divinatory arts but call them by different names. Divination is the ability to predict, foretell, or foresee or receive inspiration from a god. It attempts to achieve insight into a situation or question by using rituals or processes related to the occult or standard practice. The diviner will either make contact with some supernatural or spiritual agency or read omens, events, or signs. It can be viewed as a method to systematically organize the random and disjointed facts of existence so that they can be used to provide insight into a current problem.

In ancient Greece, both seers and oracles used the art of divination. A prophet is a person who provides prophetic precognition or prediction or insightful counsel regarding the future, using information that was supplied by data received from gods. The prophecies the oracles provided were considered to be the words that came directly from the gods. Of greater importance for the primary source of divination were the seers, since more of them were available. Seers did not speak directly to the gods, as oracles did. They interpreted signs that the gods provided. Seers used any method at their disposal to divine the word of the gods. The oracles' advantage over the seers was that the prophets could fully answer a question where a seer could only respond with yes or no answers.

Man has long had a passion for knowing their destiny, which led to divination. Divination provides answers for current events based on what happened in the past and what might happen in the future. There are countless channels for manifesting the intuition that is needed for divination.

Typing the personality of a person has been a prevalent practice in the East for centuries. Especially in Japan, revealing information about an individual's personality will give information on the person's inhibiting and productive traits, destiny, possible future parenting techniques, and compatibility regarding marriage. They often consider a person's personality as the driving factor when it comes to deciding compatibility for relationships. The Chinese swear by the Chinese zodiac signs based on the birth year of the individual matching with a particular animal. They often mix in traits of celestial types, as are found in the planets. In the East, they also have a divine personality using yin and yang, the four essential elements, and the cardinal directions. Numerology uses a different number based on numbers that are significant in a person's life, such as their date of birth or the letters in their names. Divination is accomplished with many different methods depending on the religion and the items they have available at their disposal.

TEA READING – Reading the leftover tea leaves or coffee grounds at the bottom of a cup is a complex form of divination and gives the reader numerous and different ways. The idea is to see an image and ascertain its meaning.

TAROT – While it is not known who created the first deck of Tarot cards, it is known that this is the most popular divination method, and it has been in use for centuries. Beyond their use for divination, Tarot cards are also used to connect current events and all possible connections. There are infinite combinations, and one or more will have the ability to solve all problems.

GRAINS OF CORN – Early civilizations in North and South America regularly used divination to gather knowledge. They linked the practice with the sciences of meteorology and astronomy. They were especially interested in determining when to plant certain crops and mark the calendar seasons. A unique method of divination was to use grains of corn. These corn grains are thrown onto a white cloth or a flat surface, and then the answer is determined based on the way the grains fell.

SCRYING – This is one of the oldest divination methods, and it was practiced by many of the ancient cultures. In ancient Mesopotamia, they used oil that was poured into unique bowls. The ancient Greeks looked into the reflection on metals and in mirrors. Scrying was practiced in ancient Egypt using ink. The Aztecs read thoughts in obsidian. The idea is to look into the reflection for answers to questions and desired knowledge. This ancient practice eventually led to crystal readings and the powers associated with gazing into the crystal ball.

SAND DIVINATION – Reading the shapes in the sand is one of the oldest and most beautiful forms of divination. Messages found in the sand layers were read, and this method was frequently used in ancient Muslim communities. The sand can be thrown out on a cloth or a board specially made for sand divination, and it is necessary to know the codes that the geometric figures correspond to.

Precognition and Spirituality

Precognition is the ability to know that things are going to happen before they even occur. Since ancient people's times, precognition has been associated with dream states and trances that involve such phenomena as premonitions, second sight, fortune-telling, and prophecy. Events of foreknowledge usually happen when a person receives a mental scenario in short sequences. Precognition can occur when you are awake or asleep.

You can seek answers in many different methods for your spiritual questions. If you are open enough, you will receive dialog directly from channeling that can be impactful and inspirational. Opening your heart and soul to the higher vibrations from sources outside of ordinary teachings will leave you wide open to receive the images known as precognition.

The knowledge that you seek is already inside of you, but it needs to be unlocked to enable you to have access to the information. You can remove resistance to your spiritual awareness no matter where you arrived from or where you currently are in your spiritual past. If you think you do not possess this ability if you doubt your capabilities, which are just negative information from you that seeks answers for your emotional and spiritual problems.

Precognition is part of clairvoyance. Too many people do not want to use their Third Eye or see into the future. They may fear the unknown or what they might see during their spiritual journey. If you're going to see clearly, you will need to be able to accept things that could not make any sense at that time, and you need to be able to take them without question because many of these truths will be far beyond the realm of what is believed to be possible.

Real precognition lies in collecting the details of the image you see. Anyone can see a future vision, but taking note of the elements is an integral part of the view. Precognition will provide you with a depth of understanding you never had before.

Etheric Entities on the Physical Plane

Magic and spiritual work often involve the ability to work with entities of the etheric. An etheric entity is a being that is energetic and non-material. Everyone is a multi-dimensional creature with multiple forms of their body on many different densities and activity levels. The only vehicle capable of moving through an incarnation is the physical body. Then the physical form branches out into multiple energies and fields known as the plasma body, the dream body, the astral body, the meridian body, the auric body, and the energy body. You cannot see the other planes of existence and densities' light resonant frequencies, although you can feel them. You are only able to see the physical plane of yourself.

When you begin your awakening process, you will realize that the world is basically upside down and backward from what it should be. Your new awareness will give you the need for information that will lead you to the darkness of the world and out into the light on the other side. As you search, you will encounter the entities of the etheric. These entities will vary significantly in their sentience, power, and form. Those who possess a greater complexity of etheric patterns will have greater sentience. Their influence on the etheric level is directly related to their energy levels.

You might be allowed to interact with several different forms of etheric entities. There will be deities, disembodied humans, complex spirits, cultivated spirits, and simple spirits. All of these entities are the different aspects of the multifaceted cosmos. The gods are the broader fields of power and consciousness within the etheric realm. Humans most often see them because they possess the ability to manifest themselves to humans in ways in which they can be seen. The various spirits are smaller and more localized entities within the etheric realm. They can change their form as they please. You will draw upon a larger collective of consciousness by interacting with these entities.

You will need to develop the skills required to see and communicate with them to work effectively with these entities. You will use etheric perception to become aware of their presence and etheric communication to interact with them. The type of interaction you have will depend on the nature of your goal, the relationship between you and the entity, and the type of entity you are interacting with. The reality of the etheric and the entities is entirely subject to the interpretation of your mind

CHAPTER 9
Life After Life

Man has long been fascinated by the gateway to the universe that runs through the Third Eye. Your soul will connect directly to this gateway and bring the energy of the universe to your life. Your brain and all of its components direct everything in your bodies. Your soul shines a light on the Third Eye, where the energy of the body and the mind meet as one. Pictures of saints and other holy figures show them with a golden halo of light surrounding their heads because they were aware of the goodness of their souls. Their attention was focused on their souls and the radiance that comes from the Third Eye. They operated out of that awareness that the soul was one with the mind. They achieved the climb to the peak of the sensory pyramid. Even those people who were not clairvoyant appeared with rings of radiance surrounding their heads.

Mediation allows the person who is meditating to spend time focusing on their soul. It is a process to withdraw from the body's sensations and the mind, the thought apparatus. Those who are experienced at focusing their attention on meditation can expand their focus to greater heights. They can knock on the door of heaven. Their soul will withdraw away from their body as it passes through the process of removing itself from the body. While the mind and the self are still in focus at this time, the feeling is in your emotional and spiritual body.

Elevated Souls on Earth

The advanced souls on earth have a difficult spiritual journey ahead of them. Because of the hardships they suffer, they want to spread healing and love around the world. As children, they often had no one to help them, so they wanted to help everyone. The trauma and turmoil that they suffered as children have made them into loving and giving souls.

Their job on earth is to restore humanity to a way of balance, love, and harmony. They want to alleviate the chaos in the world and restore order. They are on a spiritual path designed to make life better for themselves and the world around them. They are connected to the world in a profoundly selfless manner. They relate deeply to the entities in the world, plants, animals, and people. No matter how crazy their journeys might be, they are always peaceful and at peace.

Instead of being full of bitterness, they are still seeking a higher purpose in life. They like to spend their time helping and teaching others as they encourage self-love.

Advanced souls spend their lives trying to bring out the best in other people. They shine their lights brightly so that those in need will know who to come to for assistance. They emanate charisma and charm, and their magnetic field guides people to them. They heal hearts and souls and share their wisdom with anyone who will listen. They bring positive change to the world with their goodness and love.

Daydreams for Life

Daydreaming is the constant stream of consciousness that detaches people from their current external tasks. It directs their attention away from external items and leads them to internal and personal matters. This redirection is a common phenomenon that is almost everyone's daily lives. The various other names for daydreaming are random thoughts, fantasy, and mind wandering. Some daydreams are beneficial, and some are disruptive, and no two imaginations are identical. There are five potential positive functions that daydreaming serves: relief from boredom, dishabituation, attention cycling, creative thinking, and future thinking.

A distinct and very adaptive function of daydreaming is the relief from boredom. Daydreaming allows people to let their thoughts wander while they are doing repetitive or monotonous tasks. This wandering will not cause the external activity to be disrupted, but it will temporarily detach the person. Daydreaming does seem to make time pass better. Dishabituation is needed when the external stimulus is continuously repeated and causes a decrease in internal stimulation. This boredom happens when learning is repetitive. People learn more effectively when that learning is broken up into parts instead of given all at once. The ability to daydream lets you relieve the strain on your mind caused by intense, repetitive learning by mentally stepping away for a while, and you can return when you choose to.

An adaptive function of daydreaming is attention cycling. It helps to keep your behaviors in optimal condition when you face multiple problems at the same time. This cycling will let you choose the appropriate action for the situation when you are dealing with various situations. Daydreaming will let you switch between different thoughts and streams of information when you have many goals. Creative thinking associates daydreaming with increased creativity. If you spend some time daydreaming while trying to solve a complicated problem, you will find your most productive moments come when you are daydreaming. Intentional daydreaming is constructive when it is used in periods of intense thought.

Future thinking is also known as autobiographical thinking, which gives you the ability to anticipate and speculate about future events. It allows for better planning and the opportunity to prepare for future events and goals. It can also help keep you mind off your relevant goals while deciding on the best course of events to help you reach that goal.

Scientists and psychologists have been interested in the wanderings of the mind for years. They know that the brain has specific structures known as the default network of the brain. This network links several areas of the brain together that are involved in sensory experiences. The technical term for these impulses in the brain is the independent thoughts of the brain's stimulus. They cause the brain to think about something apart from the events coming in from outside sources. In everyday speech, the wanderings of the mind are also known as daydreams and fantasies.

Besides serving to entertain you when you are bored, daydreams serve useful purposes. They will help you to explore your inner experiences and ideas. People specifically engage their internal stimulus systems when trying to make moral or ethical decisions, understand what other people are thinking, imagine an event that might occur in the future, and contemplate their own past experiences.

It is your default network that makes your daydreaming possible. The nature of your daydreams will have a direct effect on your mind and soul. Men will dream more often when their lives are unsatisfactory. Women don't desire more often due to lower satisfaction with life, but their daydreams will become more vivid. Both men and women who daydream about friends and family members generally report being more satisfied with their lives. People who are not happy with their lives will often daydream about fictional characters or people from their past, especially in romantic situations. People who daydream like this tend to have less social support than most people and are often lonely. There are four practical ways in which you can use your daydreaming to your advantage.

- Do not allow your daydreams to interfere with what you need to do, but don't let them interfere with your creativity. You need to daydream now and then feed your imagination, but not so much that your daydreaming interferes with what you need to get done in your daily life. Make sure you are paying enough attention to experience to get done what you need to get done.
- When you need to focus, you will need to turn off your brain's default network actively. When you deactivate the system, you will have your best chance to learn new concepts and skills. So if your daydreams are getting in the way of your daily life tasks, then feel free to turn down the network's volume.
- Change your daydreams if they are not satisfying to you. Try to fantasize about the relationships that you are currently in and ways to make them better. Daydreaming about relationships that you will never have will make you more dissatisfied with your current life situation.
- Your memory can be helped or hurt by your tendency to daydream. When your daydreams keep you closer to home, your daily performance will be better than it will if your fantasies take you to places that are far away.

Daydreams are often used to reveal aspects of the personal life of an individual. Based on the details you imagine during a daydreaming episode, you will be informed about your personality. When you rehearse or replay your thoughts or actions in your mind, this is known as self-reflecting daydreaming. This form of trance can have results that are both detrimental and beneficial. You will suffer from an increase in negative thoughts if you focus too much on negative reviews from the past or imagining negative possibilities in the future. Use self-reflective daydreaming for positive imaginings, such as ways to show creativity or planning for the future. It can be beneficial for you and result in more positive thoughts.

People who are stuck in boring jobs or are unemployed are more likely to daydream than people who have exciting or at least satisfying jobs. Much like nighttime dreaming, daydreaming is when your mind will consolidate all of the information received on a specific topic or event. Brain areas that are associated with solving complex problems are highly active when people are daydreaming. So regular daydreaming might help you to achieve success in your life as you sort through your issues.

Dreaming and Symbolism

Dreams are thought to be messages from higher powers or the world of spirits. Plans often contain images and symbols that have a particular meaning in the natural world. The number of symbols or images that come to people in their dreams is countless. Suppose you can dream about something that something can carry a deeper emotional and psychological significance than just the image of the item brings. One typical image that appears in dreams is the image of a house. Different people will read other things into the appearance of a home in their goals. It might be a place they once lived, it relates to the physical body of the person, or it might hold deeper meaning if it represents something from your childhood. A house is a physical representation of your emotional and spiritual self. If you dream about a place you lived in as a child, you might be looking for a simpler and happier life. If you dream about exploring a strange house, you may be seeking change in your life. If one of the house rooms is not accessible, that might represent something in your life that you are not yet ready to examine. The way you react to the house and what you do in the dream is the key to understanding its meaning in your physical life. There is no single meaning for images and symbols seen in dreams, but some pictures of plans are so common that they carry a generally accepted definition.

- Being chased in a dream does not indicate the actual chase, but what you are running away from, which represents something you are avoiding in your life or great fear.
- Food symbolizes nourishment, knowledge, or energy and is directly related to your spirituality, emotions, and intellect. It might also mean that you are hungry for new knowledge or insights in your life.
- Dreams of water are tied to your current emotional state.
- If you dream about a baby, it doesn't necessarily mean that you want one, unless you do. Dreaming about a baby represents the desire for personal growth or professional development.
- Dreams about vehicles of any kind often reflect the direction that you think your life is going in or an obstacle that you need to face.
- Dreaming about being nude in a place where no one else is nude usually means that you feel vulnerable or fear psychological or emotional exposure.
- If you dream about different people, it reflects the various aspects of your personality.

- Death doesn't always need to be a negative omen because it means that you need to drastically change something in your life in the world of dreams.
- Falling can be the ominous sign that you need to let go of something in your life. But it can also be a serene feeling, especially if you know you need to let go of that thing.
- Adults who dream of being in the classroom are often looking for inspiration in lessons they learned in childhood.
- You might feel that you lack control over your personal life if you dream about being paralyzed.
- When you fly in your dreams, it relates to the control you feel you have over your own life, and whether you fly well or poorly correlates to your perceived level of control. Flying high indicates that you are confident and euphoric; flying low means you are frustrated or depressed.

Awareness of the Aura

Reading an aura is like looking into someone's soul because the ambiance is created from the colors that correspond to the energy that comes from the person. The atmosphere is the magnetic field of life that surrounds all living people. Every aura comprises seven layers that form one aural body, the subtle inner body's outer reflection. More energy means a more massive atmosphere, so people who have suffered in life will generally have larger auras than young or have lived a sheltered life. Clairvoyants can read the auras of people and the scenes, blockages, and energy patterns in the aura. Every color has its meaning.

The aura is made of seven bodies of energy and three planes. The spiritual plane is your connection to the divine and your intuition. The astral plane is the bridge between your spiritual plane and your physical plane and comes from the link to your heart. And the physical plane includes your mental body, emotional body, and your etheric body. The colors of your aura directly correspond to the chakras in your body. If any of the chakras are imbalanced, that will reflect on how their color displays in the aura. This reflection will tell how the person is feeling spiritually, emotionally, mentally, and physically. The aura will continuously change colors and depth of color to mirror the chakras in the person. The energy fields will attach to the person with little attachment cords. There might also be tears in the aura if different chakras are severely damaged.

The colors that are found in the aura that directly relate to the chakra are these:

- White – peace and truth – The Crown Chakra
- Purple or Indigo – wisdom and divinity – The Third Eye Chakra
- Blue or indigo – self-expression and communication – The Throat Chakra
- Green – love and nurturing – The Heart Chakra
- Yellow – intellect and self-esteem – The Solar Plexus Chakra
- Orange – ambition, and creativity – The Sacral Chakra
- Red – passion, and vitality – The Root Chakra

To perceive and accurately interpret an aura, you need to be aware of yourself enough to know the place where you end and the other person begins. If they are not, then the reading may only reflect themselves and not their perception of the other person. Spirit mediums are easily able to read auras. Reading a person's aura can help determine chakra blockages and imbalances, precognition, and determining strengths of personality and spirit.

Seeing into the Afterlife

After you leave your physical body, your identity, your stream of consciousness, will continue to reside in the astral plane. This entity might be your soul or your spirit, or even some part of your essential role. The destination that your essence takes after your death will depend on what your beliefs are in the physical plane. You may move on to take up residence for eternity in Heaven. You might be reborn into the world and begin life again with no actual memory of the experience you had before.

Everyone will die eventually. Many people fear death because there is no way to know what is beyond death in the afterlife. People have near-death experiences and describe beautiful colors, softness, and the bright light at the end of the tunnel, but that might be nothing more than the corridor that houses the end of life; it might have nothing at all to do with experience in the next world. It is assumed to be a glimpse of Heaven, but no one knows for sure.

Atheists have varying views on the afterlife. Heaven is not a viable destination for them since they do not believe in God. However, some think that there is some possibility for reincarnation or life on an astral plane. Buddhists believe in reincarnation but not in the soul. They teach that the deceased only wait a short time in a state of suspension before taking on their new form. Hindus also believe in reincarnation, and they even concede to the presence of the soul. Christian ideals depend on the denomination, but there is an abiding feeling in God and Heaven's existence as a destination for the soul after death occurs.

So the presence or absence of any form of afterlife, and what might happen there, will depend solely on what you believe will happen there when you die.

The Ascended Masters are spiritually enlightened and have moved beyond all of their incarnations in the physical realm. They have taken the Fifth Initiation and can dwell in the Fifth Dimension's heavenly kingdom. They were known as Spiritual Master, Shaman, Commoner, Guru, Yogi, or Master. When the Master is able, he will gain full union with the Mighty Presence.

As individuals on earth, the Masters learned all of the lessons of life during their incarnations. They were able to fulfill their divine plan, balance out at least fifty-one percent of their negative karma with positive karma, and gained the necessary mastery over the physical plane's limitations. In this understanding, the Ascended Master has achieved a state where he is very much like a god. His ascension has reunited him with himself in the image of the gods.

The Ascended Masters act as teachers for humanity, working from the spirit realm. They do to attend to humanity's need for spiritual assistance, and they act to motivate and inspire the spiritual growth of the individual. Anyone who wishes to achieve the rank of Ascended Master has the power to do so if they will only follow the path that begins on earth and continues through their reincarnations until they have fulfilled all of the requirements.

Reincarnation

Also known as transmigration or rebirth, reincarnation is the religious or philosophical view that the soul or spirit will begin a new life in a new form after their physical body dies. Many of the Indian religions, like Hinduism, Sikhism, Buddhism, and Jainism, teach the belief in reincarnation.

When you leave your present body and are reincarnated into a new life form, the idea is that you will strive to live better than you did in your previous life. The structure of your reincarnation will depend on how you lived in your last experience. Those who lived poorly or misbehaved will be reincarnated as something undesirable, something like a bug or a poisonous plant. Those who lived a good life would return as something more pleasant. The next life's quality in any particular incarnation will depend on the person's karma as they move through images. Someone with more negative karma than positive karma will need to continue reincarnating until rebalancing their karmic bank. This rebalancing is not used as a type of punishment but as a method of teaching. If someone's karmic balance is more negative than positive, they have not learned to let go of their ego and live righteous lives.

When a person finally learns to live the most moral incantation, they will find salvation after death. This liberation is the actual pursuit of reincarnation. Most Western ideas picture reincarnation as the desire to go back to a better life than the person will truly enjoy, but that is not true. The goal of reincarnation is to stop being reborn so that the soul will know eternal peace.

People in the west are experiencing a developing interest in reincarnation. As the ancient world's teachings become better known, people seek new answers to the world's current problems. They become more accepting of the old ideals and teachings, one of which is reincarnation. They have hundreds of years of beliefs to go through while deciding if reincarnation will be part of their new belief system. This desire to believe in life after life reinforces man's desire to find meaning and purpose in their present lives. It is difficult to accept that one day all of this will be over and we will be gone. But if we are reincarnated, we will have the chance to return to earth and do the things we couldn't do before or make amends for past wrongs. This desire gives us the motivation and vision to explore who we really are and strive to achieve the best part of yourself that you can. In doing this, we will assure ourselves the best possible life when we do return to earth in our new form to live life on earth again.

CHAPTER 10
Improved Life With An Open Third Eye

The intuition of your Third Eye binds your conscious mind with your spiritual mind. It is the spiritual you that is aware of your emotions and your experiences. Your Third Eye is a magnificent tool that brings you to deep understanding and insight. Once your Third Eye is opened, you will begin to evolve into your potential of the highest growth. Your intuition will grow strong after the Third Eye is opened, and it will be evident to you in many different situations.

People whose Third Eye chakras are open have easy access to their intuition. Whether they've reached illumination or are still moving toward it, these people have a deeper understanding of reality and the nature of the human condition. They tend to be unflappable and feel good to be around because of their relaxed personality. It isn't that they don't care. They see things from a broader perspective (the bigger picture) and understand that everything is unfolding the way it needs to; they know through personal experience that all in existence is connected. We are all extensions of divine source energy. These people don't worry because they know that all will work out for the greater good, which is true enough.

Your Third Eye has been inside your physical body since birth, waiting to connect to your spiritual self. It has always been activated and spinning. It was active in your early childhood when you had confidence and will-power, and you trusted in the truth of everyone and everything. In childhood, you were powered by life and all the dreams you had for the future. You were likely sensitive to the happenings around you, and you frequently saw entities that the adults in your life could not see. But you knew they existed, in the days before you became conditioned and no longer believed in the other world.

Developing your Third Eye will once again open the doorway to your psychic reality. It will give you the abilities you left behind in your childhood, your clairvoyance, your projection into the astral plane, and your lucid dreaming. When the Third Eye connection is cultivated, you will no longer be separated from your spirit. Metaphysical connections to the Third Eye will allow you to awaken while in the dream state and pass humanity's normal limits by walking between the realities you perceive.

Negativity comes from a blocked Third Eye, the kind of negativity that brings negative thoughts along with confusion and uncertainty. The highest source of ethereal energy comes from an open Third Eye. Your physical eyes will only see the physical world. The vision from the Third Eye connects the physical world with the spirit world. Gaining access to your Third Eye and all of its powers will give your insight and intuition as well as clarity of mind that will bring powers of concentration and decisiveness. Your Third Eye links you to enhanced imagination, astral projection, lucid dreaming and quality of sleep, and the ability to view others' aura. You will encounter visions and messages of guidance once you open your Third Eye. Use your strength and follow through on what is offered by your intuition, and the strength of your Third Eye will deepen and develop.

It is normal for humans to reach early adulthood carrying with them the fears of the future that bring anxiety and depression. Once the awareness of the spiritual world closes, at about age six, humans become mired in the illusion of their own ego and the pursuit of materialism. Your systems of belief and education will be destroyed when you open your Third Eye. Truth and enlightenment will come to you when you throw off the restraints of old beliefs and ideals. This will prove to be the hardest obstacle to your awakening because you will need to leave all of your old systems of comfort to gain the truth that is waiting for you. When you release that fear of what will happen to you and who you will become, you will then ease into the fields of contentment and compassion that your intuition is always guiding you towards.

In the beginning, your ego will reject the discipline and focus that you are trying to teach yourself. Your ego will go to great lengths to distract you since it needs to keep you away from the picture of the perfect world that you are attempting to grow toward. It is through the process of surrender to the wisdom of your Third Eye that your life will unfold. That will allow you to gain the greater truth of reality. You will then know that all is well as you bask in your new feelings of self-assuredness.

Your new sense of knowing and understanding will lead you down your new path in life. Even during tough times in your life, you will know what to do and how to proceed. The truth will grow in your mind and heart as you begin to view life more clearly. The illusions of the ego will no longer hold you back. Your childhood abilities will return to aid you in your adult life.

When you open your Third Eye, you enter a massive field of energy. You will access higher planes of consciousness and different astral planes as you realize you are no longer chained by your body and your mind. The new knowledge that love, joy, and peace come from within will surprise and delight you.

Learning to use the field of energy is one of the fun effects of opening your Third Eye. The subtle areas of energy that your physical eyes can't see will be apparent in your intuitive center. This field of life is fueled by your thoughts, intentions, and emotions. All living creatures have their own field of vibration. You will realize the connection between your energy field and the energy emitted by other beings and entities.

You will realize you are not just your body, mind, and emotions, and this more profound realization is called inner knowing. Deep meditation will help you arrive at this state. Your intuition will bring you to this realization. You are not just a product of the components of your physical body, feelings, or thoughts, and you are far above the influence of material things. Your intuitive senses prove that you are aware of yourself, experienced, and witness of experiences. You will witness your emotions, thoughts, and spiritual and physical sensations. You will become one with your experiences with this awareness of your attention.

You will access higher planes of consciousness and know ascended masters, deities, guardian angels, spirit guides, Buddha, Jesus. Every ascended master becomes directly accessible to those on earth. The world of the ascended spirits and the astral planes' universal wisdom is yours when your intuition opens. When used with the simple intention, you can connect with these guides and helpers to assist you on your path. Whether that is through divination or receiving healing and support, they will help you along your way.

You will learn that joy, love, and peace are not found outside of you. Most people seek these spiritual pleasures from the attention of other people. These are temporary springs your intuition will guide you away from. You will learn that everything you need will be found inside of you. You will leave behind the constant pursuit of earthly desires that make you suffer from your wanting and searching. You will learn to seek the bottomless well of calm and peace found within you.

You will surrender to the depth within you. Your intuitive awakening will benefit you immediately in beautiful ways after opening your Third Eye. You will have the power to access parts of yourself that might once have been hidden from you.

Your fear of the unknown might haunt you while opening your Third Eye, but this fear will fade as you grow stronger in your energies. As your thoughts direct your energy, if you feel fear, you will create a negative experience during your awakening because of that fear. You will gain access to the depths of love within your own love and enjoy the experience of the awakening. Your mind and heart will determine the speed of your awakening. The more you trust your personal decision and surrender your ego, the more powerfully you will connect.

With your increased intuition and clairvoyant and telepathic abilities, you will desire a more meaningful life. You will need to create an experience more connected to your higher purpose. All souls begin life on earth with their divine mission preprogrammed inside. With your open Third Eye, you will face your true calling and seek your divine mission. Everything new inside you will prompt you to make needed changes. You will seek more meaningful relationships, and you will devote more of your time to pursuits that are meaningful for you. You will seek jobs and activities that will allow you to make a change in the world. You will experience the exalted freedom that comes with eternal love for yourself.

CONCLUSION

Thank you for coming to the end of *Open Your Third Eye*. Let's hope this book was interesting and informative and able to give you all of the tools you will need to achieve all of your goals, no matter what they may be.

The next step is to open your Third Eye and begin your journey to the path of enlightenment and self-realization. Your Third Eye is your doorway to the world beyond the physical world that your physical eyes see. Third Eye vision will put you in touch with all of the powers of the universe and all of the images that were locked to you before. You will have access to astral planes and other worlds. Beings that inhabit these planes will come to you in a fantastic display of connection and awareness.

The beings that will come to you have always been with you, but your open Third Eye will give you greater access to them. You will experience elevated states of consciousness that will increase your psychic abilities and your spirituality. You will learn methods for emptying your mind and truly relax with the power of meditation that enables freedom for your mind.

The power of mysticism will now be open to you. With that will come an ability to develop your automatic writing and extrasensory perception. You may find a new career as a medium, channeling the departed thoughts into forms that are easy for those left behind to comprehend. An open Third Eye will cause you to desire life more accessible to others, with ways in which you can assist others. This channeling might be your new calling in life.

You will also develop control over your dreams, allowing you to indulge in out of body experiences with people from other astral planes. Through the powers of divination, you will enable your powers of precognition. You will also find communications with beings who have gone before so that you can better understand the life beyond life known as reincarnation.

Finally, if you found this book was useful to you in any way, a review on Amazon is always appreciated!

DESCRIPTION

Do you ever feel as though there must be more to life than what you are currently experiencing? Is something important missing in your life? Do you ever desire to be more intuitive, more aware, or more in touch with yourself and the world around you? Is your life lacking something warm and vital? If any of this sounds like you and how you are currently feeling, then you are in the best place to find the answers you need.

It is so easy to get trapped in the merry-go-round of life, never really enjoying the ride but not knowing how to get off the ride. You know there is a better life waiting for you, but you are not sure how to find it. Life should be full of more importance than the one you are currently living in. You feel out of touch with the world around you, and you would like to get back some of the warmth and love you might have known long ago. Or maybe you have never known those feelings and would like to begin to enjoy them.

Open Your Third Eye is the book that you need in your life to help you reach the goals you need to achieve for the life you want to live. Your Third Eye is the basis of your spiritual world and the key to opening the divine life you desire. With your Third Eye open and activated, you will know the peace and understanding of the universe that has been missing in your life. And this is the book that will show you how to achieve that peace. You will learn to:

- Meditate for peace and calm
- Utilize crystals and essential oils
- Open your consciousness to guidance from divine beings
- Let go of your ego to allow your spirit to soar

Opening your Third Eye takes time and attention, and there may be some fear along the way. You will need to allow yourself to let go of your ego, that part of you that holds onto old beliefs and ideals that might be holding you back. When you can admit that these things are preventing you from living the life you want to live, you will be ready for the spiritual enlightenment that comes with an open Third Eye. You will be able to experience:

- ESP

- Psychic sense and abilities
- Mediumistic channeling
- Travel on astral planes
- Telepathic awareness

You will know the ability to communicate with those beings from other astral planes. You will see how to control your dreams so that you can experience out of body travel to other astral planes. You will attain the ability to know and see your guardian angels and other spirit guides on earth and learn how important they are to your health and well-being. And you will see that an open Third Eye will relieve your fears about life after this life ends and how your spirit can go on after the body has gone.

All of this, and more, will enable you to open your Third Eye and achieve all of the goals and dreams you have kept buried all these years. You will know true peace and self-realization. Buy this book, and begin the journey to your new life today.

www.ingramcontent.com/pod-product-compliance
Lightning Source LLC
Chambersburg PA
CBHW081348070526
44578CB00005B/769